IN HONOUR OF THE VISIT OF

HIS MAJESTY
SULTAN QABOOS BIN SAID

GERMAN UNIVERSITY OF TECHNOLOGY IN OMAN
GUTECH – THE FIRST TEN YEARS (2007–2017)

Edited by
Michael Jansen, Michael Modigell
and Burkhard Rauhut

Georg Olms Verlag
Hildesheim · Zürich · New York
2020

Bibliographic information published by Die Deutsche Nationalbibliothek
Die Deutsche Nationalbibliothek lists this publication in the Deutsche Nationalbibliografe; detailed bibliographic data are available on the Internet at http://dnb.d-nb.de

Concept and Visualization: Michael Jansen

Final Editing: Michaela Liehner-Jansen

Cover design and typesetting: Weiß-Freiburg GmbH – Grafik und Buchgestaltung

Printed on durable and acid-free paper

Printed in Germany

© GUtech & Editors

Photos © GUtech & Editors

except pp. 10, 13, 14, 117–120 by Hoehler + alSalmy (H+S),

and p.114 by GERMAN DESIGN AWARD/https://www.german-design-award.com

© Georg Olms Verlag AG, Hildesheim 2020

All rights reserved

www.olms.de

(luxury edition) ISBN 978-3-487-15946-1

(regular edition) ISBN 978-3-487-15673-6

His Majesty Sultan Haitham bin Tarik Al Said, enthroned on January 11, 2020. He honoured GUtech with his visit on the occasion of the Inauguration Ceremony of the History of Science Centre on December 28, 2017.

TABLE OF CONTENTS

Chapter 6 — Greetings

Chapter 7 — Excursions

Chapter 8 — Special Events

Chapter 9 — Graduation Ceremonies

Appendix — List of Authors

CHAPTER 1
INTRODUCTION

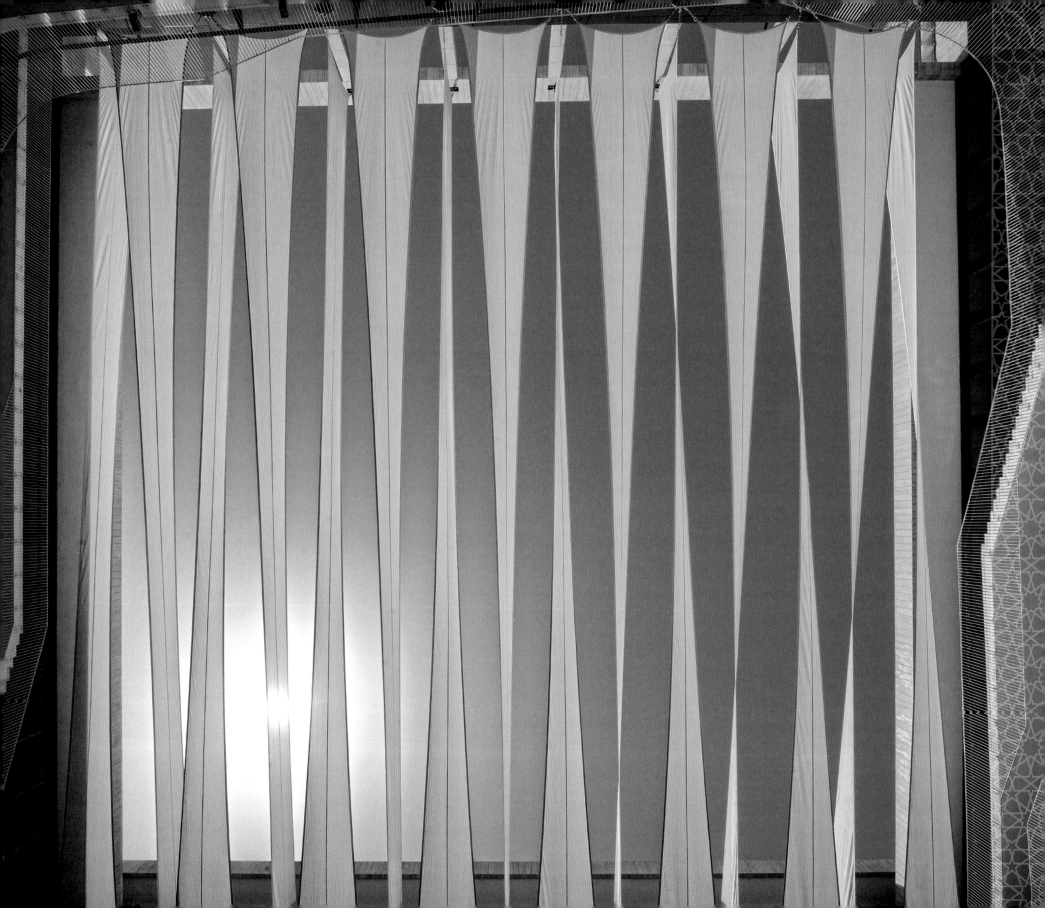

FOREWORD

The visit of His Majesty Sultan Qaboos bin Said on 24th December 2012 to the German University of Technology in Oman, GUtech, will remain the highlight of all endeavours, not only for those who have been engaged in the founding and establishment of the University, but also for the youth of Oman pursuing their education at GUtech.

Therefore the 24th of December 2012 marks this historic event of happiness and joy, and has thus been declared a GUtech holiday to remember the Visit of His Majesty Sultan Qaboos bin Said.

The visit of His Majesty Sultan Qaboos bin Said in 2012 marked the fifth year of academic activities at GUtech.

Ten years earlier, in 2002, the idea of founding a university was born by the Omani stakeholders and two professors of RWTH Aachen University, followed by preparatory work at RWTH. The official application to the Ministry of Higher Education to found the university received a positive response on 30th June 2006. The final signing of the cooperative agreement between Oman Educational Services LLC (OES) and the Rheinisch-Westfälische Technische Hochschule Aachen (RWTH) took place in Muscat on 26th December 2006.

On 12th December 2017, the fifth anniversary of the visit of His Majesty Sultan Qaboos bin Said and the tenth anniversary of the beginning of university life was celebrated in the new university campus of Halban along with the inauguration of the new History of Science Centre on 28th of December 2017.

The road undertaken up until today has been marked by an accelerated growth stemming from the initial interim campus in Al Athaiba with the 'Beach Villas'. These first buildings, which hosted the University for almost 4 years, overlook the Arabian Sea and as a good omen have safely survived the destructive force of cyclone Gonu in June 2007.

As GUtech expanded in numbers, the beach villas proved too small in space. In 2010 the campus was moved to a high-rise building, the so-called 'Airport Campus' with more space and a view overlooking the highway and the new airport which was under construction at the time. Large banners with the image of His Majesty could be seen hanging on the façade on special occasions; an impressive view for passers-by driving on Sultan Qaboos Highway.

Meanwhile the land for the construction of the university campus had been granted and in 2012 the building designed by a group of architects, all alumni from RWTH Aachen University, was completed.

Within only 20 months the new complex with an architecture markedly extravagant in its design was finalized, and the university moved, for the third time, to its final destination, the Halban Campus. The new Halban building has since then been honoured with many awards for its architectural eminence.

Today the piazza in front of the main building is framed to its south by the solitary architecture of the History of Science Centre and to its north by another building hosting the Faculty of Urban Planning and Architectural Design as well as the laboratories of other faculties. Behind the main building there are residential buildings to house students and staff and until recently the Campus has also hosted the Finland Oman School (FOS) which is committed to providing teaching from Kindergarten level up.

Reading through the book is a journey through GUtech's history, from its very beginning up until today.

The first dedication of this volume goes to His Majesty the Sultan of Oman, who has consistently supported education in his country and who constantly emphasizes the need of (higher) education, especially for young Omani women. Therefore, one of the central endeavours of the German University of Technology in Oman is to provide the young generation of Oman with the technical and moral know-how for the future of the country to support the further establishment of a platform for a modern economy in a globalized world.

With the founding of GUtech, which is affiliated to RWTH Aachen University, the leading visionaries are keen to fulfil the visions of His Majesty Sultan Qaboos bin Said and Oman.

Education at GUtech has always been accompanied by the joy of learning, by the cultivation for a culture of mutual respect and by respecting the mission, vision and goals which were first formulated as early as 2004.

This fairly short time span of only fifteen years since the idea took shape, along with the preparatory phase mainly at RWTH Aachen University has been made enriching by the many who helped to build up what is existing today. A special mention goes to the founding team as well as to the founding deans, all professors of RWTH Aachen University, who have worked closely with the Omani Institutions to finalize the curricula of the first four faculties, implemented in 2007, namely the faculties of Economics and Sustainable Tourism, Engineering, Urban Planning and Architectural Design and Sciences.

Our special thanks go to the owners of GUtech which since its first shaping has been managed by Oman Educational Services LLC (OES). Their ambitious goals, based on the reputable RWTH Aachen University standards, are and will be the permanent demand of highest international standards in education.

May this book be held as a reminder and a time capsule of the power of a vision and its translation to a remarkable journey of growth towards the continuous development of Oman.

The editing committee of Rectors:

Michael Jansen (2007–2008), Burkhard Rauhut (2008–2013), Michael Modigell (2013–2020)

MESSAGE

His Excellency Sheikh Abdullah bin Mohammed Al Salmi,
Chairman of Oman Educational Services LLC (OES) since 2007

On the 24th December 2012, His Majesty Sultan Qaboos bin Said paid an honourable visit to the German University of Technology in Oman, GUtech's complex in Halban. Since then, the University has celebrated the GUtech University day on December 24th to commemorate the esteemed visit of His Majesty marking the achievement and progress made by GUtech since the academic commencement in 2007.

The idea behind the German University of Technology in Oman was inspired by several factors. The first of these was the recognition that basic and higher education are priority areas for the future progress of a nation and its people. In this respect Oman's education sector during the era of the Renaissance has already taken enormous strides forward thanks to His Majesty the Sultan's initiatives and the tireless attention he has devoted to it. Even so, the system needs to be constantly upgraded and reinforced in response to the demands of the Renaissance.

The second factor was the success story exemplified by Germany, where scientific education in theoretical and applied fields saw an impressive upsurge after the Second World War and was accompanied by the emergence of a thriving and advanced economy. It therefore made perfect sense that our thoughts should turn to the idea of a partnership with a recognised German technological university — an idea which bore fruit with the establishment of a relationship with RWTH Aachen University, one of the leading technical universities in the field of engineering and technology.

The third factor was the religious and moral motivation that inspires people to serve their community. This is the general intention behind the establishment of the *waqf* (endowment) system in Islam, or what the *fuqaha'* (Muslim jurists) call *ihtisab* ('seeking reward for good deeds'). In our society endowments for learning and establishing schools have traditionally been one of the main aims of *ihtisab* and the most instrumental in promoting education and scientific and social progress.

The fourth factor was the fact that we come from a family with a tradition of learning and hard work and undertaking this mission has given us a deep sense of satisfaction and achievement, while reaffirming our trust in Allah and our relationship with those around us. Actions are determined by their intentions.

As we mark the fifth jubilee of His Majesty's honourable visit and tenth anniversary of the foundation of the German University of Technology in Oman, our achievements over the years show that our efforts were blessedly justified. They include the graduation of successive batches of students, as well as improved, expanded and upgraded institutions, facilities and services, and new prospects for further growth for the benefit of future generations.

In asking God the Almighty to grant us continued success in our future endeavours, we would also like to extend our gratitude to the academic staff and the University administration for their unflagging contributions. Our special thanks go to our German friends and founding supporters and to RWTH Aachen University of Technology.

It is with great sadness that we bid farewell to His Majesty Sultan Qaboos bin Said Al Said, who left us on 10th of January 2020. He will always continue to live in our hearts as we cherish his wise and visionary leadership, not only as the founder of the modern Renaissance of Oman, but also as a patron to GUtech by being the driving force behind the education and enlightenment of our nation.

We warmly welcome His Majesty Sultan Haitham bin Tarik Al Said, enthroned on the 11th of January 2020, and extend our cordial gratitude for his continued support towards GUtech from its earliest days.

MESSAGE

Prof. Dr. Ernst Schmachtenberg, Rector of RWTH Aachen University 2008–2018; Chairman of GUtech Board of Governors 2008–2018

I would like to take this opportunity to congratulate GUtech on the occasion of its 10th anniversary. It is a very special university, built as a bridge between the Arabic and the European world. The bridgeheads of this university are located at Muscat and Aachen for very good reasons: I have experienced Oman as an open-minded and future-oriented country. Therefore I was convinced of the possibility of establishing a University of Technology in this country which would be able to transfer the technological science developed over centuries in Europe to the Arab world, something for which RWTH Aachen University is especially renowned in Germany.

The aim of this initiative was to give GUtech its own identity. The idea of all parties involved was not simply to create a spin-off or offshoot of RWTH Aachen University. The new institution should be firmly rooted in the culture and the society of Oman but at the same time the university should open the door for young people to be educated as engineers, natural scientists or computer scientists.

It is quite obvious that our way of thinking is very much shaped by our national, religious and societal context. Moreover, it is deeply marked by the kind of academic education we are used to. In this sense we have really tried to establish something new. Are we achieving our goal of creating Omani engineers?

Today we witness a capable university with around 2000 students. We learn from the success of our graduates that the education provided by GUtech offers them a good start in their professional life in Oman or a continuing academic career within the international system. As Chairman of the Board of Governors I would like to congratulate all those who have contributed to this success.

I would like to mention in particular three very important people who made this success possible: The first one is His Excellency Sheikh Abdullah bin Mohammed Al Salmi, Minister of Awqaf and Religious Affairs in Oman, who enabled the establishment and the operation of GUtech by providing the necessary material resources. His continuing engagement is the material basis of GUtech. The second one is Prof. Dr. Michael Jansen, Professor of Urban History at RWTH Aachen University, who together with Sheikh Abdullah promoted the idea of a University of Technology in Oman, organised the first feasibility study and worked as Acting Rector in 2007. The third one is Prof. Dr. Burkhard Rauhut, former Rector of RWTH Aachen University, who took over the rectorship of GUtech in 2008, running GUtech until 2013. For me personally he played a central role regarding the successful development of GUtech over the last ten years.

The project GUtech could only succeed because people with a lot of knowledge and influence from both cultural areas worked closely together. Nowadays I consider GUtech well on track since the same principle is still as valid as it was at the beginning: People in the management of GUtech, both from Germany and from Oman, are working closely together, with great expertise and with great commitment, to ensure the successful future development of this university.

As Chairman of the Board of Governors I wish our Omani sister institution every success in the future.

MESSAGE

Prof. Dr. Michael Modigell, Rector of GUtech 2013–2020

The 10ᵗʰ anniversary of GUtech and the fifth anniversary of His Majesty Sultan Qaboos' visit to GUtech in 2012: a unique coincidence of two important events! GUtech is proud and happy to celebrate both events this year, together with our Omani and German friends and supporters.

More than ten years ago professors of the German RWTH University Aachen started to design GUtech according to German higher education traditions and institutional experience, following the explicit wish of the sponsors of GUtech, in particular His Excellency Sheikh Abdullah bin Mohammed Al Salmi. Consequently, GUtech has the word 'German' in its name. But GUtech does not feel and behave like a foreign institution in Oman. It is important to recognise that GUtech feels it is an inherent part of the Oman educational system. This is documented by the countless activities for the community undertaken by GUtech. Anyone who has the chance to join the GUtech celebration of the National Day will see for themselves how proud GUtech students and staff are, whether Omani or international, to be part of Oman society. This has been especially documented by the visit of His Majesty five years ago. Up to now GUtech is the only private university in Oman ever visited by His Majesty. GUtech is proud of the attention His Majesty has bestowed on it and the advice and suggestions provided by His Majesty are carefully followed.

The history of GUtech is a process of continuous growth, in the number of students, the number of staff, and in the number of programmes. Starting with about 50 students ten years ago, GUtech has now nearly 2000, corresponding to a mean growth rate of around 200 students per year. Consequently the procedures, rules and organisation have had to be adjusted and modified continuously. All members of the university have been involved in this process, both academic and administrative staff. I am proud to say that this constant transformation process has worked without noticeable friction due to the commitment and engagement of all staff members.

GUtech is now at a stage where it can become a full university. Hopefully, Master programmes in all departments will start this year and a proposal for PhD programmes is in the process of being approved by the Ministry for Higher Education. A new era in the development of GUtech is beginning, and it will be exciting to follow it over the next 10 years.

At this point I want to thank all friends and supporters who contributed to the successful story of GUtech, both here in Oman and in Germany and other countries. I would personally like to thank our Board of Directors who have been so patient with us and who have always shared our vision for the future of GUtech.

Let me close with a quote by Albert Einstein, the inimitable German scientist: 'Education is not the learning of facts, but the training of the mind to think', which perfectly describes the idea of GUtech both today and in the future.

THE BLESSED VISIT OF HIS MAJESTY SULTAN QABOOS TO THE UNIVERSITY IN 2012

Abdulrahman Al Salimi, Member of Oman Educational Services LLC (OES) Executive Board since 2007

Ever since the first days of the Renaissance under His Majesty the Sultan's leadership in the 1970s, education has been the cornerstone of His Majesty's priorities. It has not just been limited to the introduction of new and updated programmes and syllabi; indeed, the whole development process has also come to incorporate what we might perhaps describe as that 'high moral spirit', which coincides with His Majesty's view that education and learning are a fundamental part of the Omani character and a basic pillar of the Blessed Renaissance.

The new nation-state created by His Majesty has always demanded broad popular participation, which is only possible if people have the necessary skills and capabilities. These are acquired through a combination of formal education, knowledge and those other human qualities that empower a person to contribute effectively to the major task of national development.

Recognising that during the era of His Majesty's Blessed Renaissance those vital human qualities needed to be combined with knowledge and an ability to participate in the development process, the state responded with a massive educational programme across the length and breadth of the Sultanate. A natural consequence of this was that Oman became a pioneer in creating an altogether new educational system, and from the early 1990s thoughts began to turn towards how to further support the state's efforts and move forward in a way that was more in line with His Majesty the Sultan's thinking.

As a result the education system in the Sultanate was upgraded from basic education through to university level, and

FIG. 1/12:
His Majesty Sultan Qaboos bin Said arriving at Halban Campus on 24th December 2012.

now—two decades later—we have come to recognise that it has produced new ways of thinking and new practices.

His Majesty has been closely monitoring the progress of the University from its earliest days and he has given us his constant encouragement and support. Even so, we must admit that we were amazed when he expressed a desire to visit the University as one of the fruits of his Renaissance which has brought progress to Oman and the Arab region.

On 24th December 2012 His Majesty graced the Omani-German University with a visit, during which he was briefed on its facilities, specialist academic disciplines and future plans and inquired about the achievements of its academic staff and students. Following his visit, he continued to inquire, put forward suggestions and give directives—to us as well as to others—thus demonstrating that he cherishes all these academic, scientific and educational enterprises as important elements in the country's overall development.

Now, as the University enters its tenth year, we have much to be proud of and much that is still a work in progress. While we have succeeded in attracting science and technology students from within the Sultanate, the Arabian Peninsula and the Indian Ocean region, the University is first and foremost an environment and milieu, and indeed, over the past two decades the Omani environment has been the most congenial in the region, thanks to the wise leadership of the Builder of this Blessed Renaissance, the stability and security he has helped spread across the region and his quiet but confident endeavours to create a promising future. We in the German Technical University in Oman are aware of His Majesty's concern and support and the fatherly critical eye he keeps upon us, and this gives us further motivation and incentives to strive for ever higher educational standards in Oman and the region. And as we are in a central location, we have become the nucleus of a constructive partnership to build a prosperous future through advanced education.

As we mark the fifth anniversary of His Majesty's visit to the university and the tenth anniversary of its foundation, we have the honour to express our sincere appreciation to the Pioneer and Leader of the Renaissance and offer him our deepest gratitude for gracing us with his visit. We ask our God to continue to grant us the blessings of His Majesty's leadership, care and support, both for us here at the University and for our society and the state. He is the One who hears and answers our prayers.

FIG. 2/12:
Visit of His Majesty Sultan
Qaboos bin Said to GUtech.

FIG. 3/12:
His Majesty Sultan Qaboos bin Said arriving at GUtech
on 24th December 2012.

FIG. 4/12:
His Majesty Sultan Qaboos bin Said greeting Sheikh Abdullah bin Salim Al Salmi, OES Board of Directors.

FIG. 5/12:
His Majesty Sultan Qaboos bin Said greeting Dr. Abdulrahman Al Salimi, OES Board of Directors.

FIG. 6/12:
His Majesty Sultan Qaboos bin Said greeting Prof. Dr. Burkhard Rauhut, GUtech Rector.

FIG. 7/12:
His Majesty Sultan Qaboos bin Said greeting Dr. Judith Rauhut, GUtech Consultant.

FIG. 8/12:
His Majesty Sultan Qaboos bin Said greeting Prof. Dr. Michael Jansen, GUtech Founding Rector.

FIG. 9/12:
His Majesty Sultan Qaboos bin Said greeting Mrs Michaela Liehner-Jansen.

FIG. 10/12:
His Majesty Sultan Qaboos bin Said greeting Dr. Hussain Al Salmi, Deputy Rector for Administration and Finance.

FIG. 11/12:
His Majesty Sultan Qaboos bin Said greeting Mohamed bin Sulaiman Al Salmi, Head of Infrastructure.

FIG. 12/12:
His Majesty Sultan Qaboos greeting Richard Lisker, Architect and Project Director of Hoehler + Partner (H+P) for GUtech, Halban Campus.

FIG. 13/12:
His Majesty Sultan Qaboos bin Said greeting Muhammad bin Sultan Al Salmy, Managing Partner and Lead Architect of Hoehler + Partner (H+P) for GUtech, Halban Campus.

FIG. 14/12:
His Majesty Sultan Qaboos bin
Said arriving at Halban Campus
on 24th December 2012.

FIG. 15/17:
GUtech's magnificent march to success culminated in the historic royal visit of His Majesty Sultan Qaboos bin Said to the new campus on 24th December 2012. The royal visit was considered to be the true inauguration of GUtech and it gave the University extra impetus to position itself to achieve the ambitious targets set for this great project.

Presentation of an Honorary Medal to the Minister of the Diwan of the Royal Court His Excellency Khalid bin Hilal Al Busaidi by His Excellency Sheikh Abdullah bin Mohammed Al Salmi.

CELEBRATING THE FIFTH ANNIVERSARY OF HIS MAJESTY'S VISIT TO GUTECH AND THE 10TH ANNIVERSARY OF THE UNIVERSITY

His Excellency Sheikh Abdullah bin Salim Al Salmi, Member of Oman Educational Services LLC (OES) Executive Board since 2007

Proudly celebrating 10 glorious years in the Sultanate, the German University of Technology in Oman (GUtech) has become one of the leading and fastest growing educational institutions in Oman.

This dream initiative was started by people who were determined to help in building this splendid nation and to contribute to the march of development led by His Majesty Sultan Qaboos bin Said. They firmly believed that a modern nation grows through increased productivity founded on knowledge, skills and high quality education. This dream became a reality when the founders decided to establish the **German University of Technology in Oman (GUtech),** a new educational institution they envisioned as becoming a leading university of technology in Oman in defining the very highest standards in education, research and innovation. GUtech developed its curricula, programmes, knowledge, know-how transfer and quality assurance through affiliation and collaboration with RWTH Aachen University.

Firstly, a *Memorandum of Understanding* was signed by His Excellency Sheikh Abdullah bin Mohammed Al Salmi and Professor Rauhut, Rector of RWTH Aachen to establish a university focusing on bringing German excellence in education and research to Oman.

Soon after this the process of obtaining Ministry of Higher Education approval started, along with the task of finding a suitable site for the campus of the newly established university. A licence to operate was granted to GUtech by the Ministry of Higher Education on 15.03.2007 after an academic partnership agreement was signed with RWTH Aachen in Muscat on 27.12.2006.

GUtech began operation in rented villas in the Shatee Athaiba area, with a small faculty and administrative team offering five academic programmes in engineering.

After three years the University had expanded its operations and programmes considerably, and after registering a significant growth in the number of students it moved to a new location next to Muscat International Airport. Its reputation as the number one private University in Oman began to gain public momentum due to its focus on, and commitment to, the provision of quality education.

Moving into its state-of-the-art permanent campus in Halban was a quantum leap for GUtech, apart from also being a major milestone in its history. Designed to offer all facilities at one location, the new campus has helped promote a first-of-its-kind professional educational ambience in the Sultanate.

GUtech's new home was designed by Hoehler + alSalmy (H+S), a renowned Omani-German engineering consultancy. H+S left no stone unturned to ensure that the new campus could fulfil the needs of both the University and its students, and worked round the clock to meet the project's strict delivery timeframe.

Ten years of high hopes, determination and perseverance have enabled GUtech to overcome all challenges and to advance at a confident pace towards achieving its desired objectives. Looking at what has been achieved so far, we remain confident that we have still more to offer our beloved nation.

We thank Almighty God for all the graces and blessing bestowed on us. We would like to express our gratitude to His Majesty Sultan Qaboos bin Said and his wise government for all the support and guidance given to us, without which we would not have been able to realise these remarkable achievements. Our special and sincere thanks go to the Ministry of Higher Education and to all the other ministries, government organisations and individuals who have offered their valuable support and who have accompanied the University on its journey to success over the last decade. Lastly, we ought not to forget to thank our German friends at RWTH Aachen and DAAD for their continued support.

FIG. 16/17:
The Minister of the Diwan of the Royal Court His Excellency
Khalid bin Hilal Al Busaidi arriving at GUtech Halban Campus
with (from left) His Excellency Sheikh Abdullah bin Salim Al Salmi
and His Excellency Sheikh Abdullah bin Mohammed Al Salmi.

FIG. 17/17:
Ceremony of the 5th Anniversary of His Majesty´s Visit to GUtech and the 10th Anniversary of the University. From left: His Highness Sayyid Kamil bin Fahad Al Said, His Excellency Khalid bin Hilal Al Busaidi, His Excellency Sheikh Abdullah bin Mohammed Al Salmi.

FIG. 18/17: Left:
Honorable address by Dr. Abdulrahman Al Salimi,
OES Board of Directors.

FIG. 19/17: Below:
Guests attending the Ceremony of the 5th Anniversary of
His Majesty's Visit to GUtech and the 10th Anniversary
of the University.
From left: German Embassy 1st Counsellor Joachim Düster,
Provost of Aachen Cathedral Manfred von Holtum, Bishop
of Aachen Dr. Heinrich Mussinghoff, Prof. Dr. Ekkehard
Holzbecher, DAAD Representative Dr. Stephan Geifes, Prof.
Dr. Barbara Stäuble, Architect Ernst Höhler, Prof. Dr. Michael
Jansen, Prof. Dr. Burkhard Rauhut.

FIG. 20/17: Left above:
The Minister of the Diwan of the Royal Court His Excellency Khalid bin Hilal Al Busaidi presenting an Honorary Medal to Founding Rector Prof. Dr. Michael Jansen.

FIG. 21/17: Left below:
The Minister of the Diwan of the Royal Court His Excellency Khalid bin Hilal Al Busaidi presenting an Honorary Medal to former Deputy Rector for Academic Affairs Prof. Dr. Barbara Stäuble.

FIG. 22/17: Above:
The Minister of the Diwan of the Royal Court His Excellency Khalid bin Hilal Al Busaidi presenting an Honorary Medal to former GUtech Rector Prof. Dr. Burkhard Rauhut.

Partially visible background text (behind photo):

... e from RWTH Aachen University in 1970.
...t the age of 28, Ernst with anoth...
...g, Germany, where their firs...established "Höhler and
...ls to be scattered throughout th...ect was to design and
...pany was then rebranded...ermany.
...ined more partners with...+ partner architects and
...artner, Muscat was esta...
...ogy, Oman (GUtech) pr...pervising the German
...g the Muscat offic...
...er, Ernst has worked wit...
...er, Henning Larsen and...
...ompleted projects aro...iophilharmonie,
...ort and the biggest m...Djazair as well as
...y of Technology, Oma...enter.

FIG. 23/17:
The Minister of the Diwan of the Royal Court His Excellency Khalid bin Hilal Al Busaidi presenting an Honorary Medal to Architect Ernst Höhler.

FIG. 24/17:
The Minister of the Diwan of the Royal Court His Excellency Khalid bin Hilal Al Busaidi presenting an Honorary Medal to DAAD Representative Dr. Stephan Geifes.

FIG. 25/17:
The Minister of the Diwan of the Royal Court His Excellency Khalid bin Hilal Al Busaidi presenting an Honorary Medal to Al Roya Editor in Chief Honourable Hatim Al Taie.

FIG. 26/17:
5th Anniversary of His Majesty's Visit to GUtech. Chief guests from right:
His Highness Sayyid Kamil bin Fahad Al Said, the Minister of Higher Education
Her Excellency Dr. Rawya bint Saud Al Busaidi, the German Ambassador
to the Sultanate of Oman His Excellency Thomas Friedrich Schneider,
GUtech Rector Prof. Dr. Michael Modigell.

FIG. 27/03:
His Excellency Sheikh Abdullah bin Mohammed Al Salmi with
the RWTH initiators of GUtech Prof. Dr. Burkhard Rauhut
and Prof. Dr. Michael Jansen.

CHAPTER 2
THE FORMATION

THE PRELUDE – HOW IT ALL BEGAN

Prof. Dr. Michael Jansen, Acting Rector of GUtech 2007–2008;
Member of GUtech Board of Governors (BoG) 2007–2012,
Full Professor of GUtech since 2012

It is rare that a private donor invites a university to participate in the founding of a new academic institution of the highest quality in his home country, yet in 2003 this is what happened to RWTH Aachen University (RWTH) in Oman.

Initiated by the advisor for Oman to the Senate of RWTH, Prof. Dr. Michael Jansen on 10th October 2003, the Al Salmi Family signed a Memorandum of Understanding with the Rector of RWTH, Prof. Dr. Burkhard Rauhut, agreeing on mutual exchange prior to establishing a private technical university in Oman based on RWTH quality standards.

The vision of a joint German-Omani university had been strongly motivated by the wish to contribute to the further economic development of Oman. Whilst other projects had already been started, this joint project was to target the development of further production capacities in Oman. Hence from the very beginning the decision of the owners was to found a technical university. These thoughts, together with personal connections, brought them to Aachen and into contact with RWTH. In order to realise the primary vision of a university offering master, post-master and post-doctoral studies with research facilities it turned out to be essential at first to set up adequate bachelor programmes. Preparatory work began as early as 2004 with a *Conception for the establishment of a university in Oman* soon to be followed by a *Draft Concept for the pre-feasibility study of first analyses and interpretation of statistical data regarding study profiles in the Sultanate of Oman, the neighbouring countries and other comparable international universities.*

Based on these first research results, on March 31st 2004 the *Letter of Intent* was signed between the Rector of RWTH and the owners:

'After according accreditation by the Oman Government Aachen University RWTH will agree to provide academic advice, supervise and monitor the academic programmes, and approve award certificates issued by the private university'.

In April 2004 it was followed by a *Draft Concept for a pre-feasibility study for the establishment of a private university with a RWTH charter in Oman.* Amongst other points, it comprised an analysis of the education potential in Oman (§2), an analysis of RWTH Aachen University education programmes (§3), an analysis of financial issues (§4), and a time-frame (§5).

In October 2004 a first architectural space-function programme for the future university buildings had been worked out by Professor Jansen, Advisor for Oman to the Senate RWTH, and his team; this also became the subject basis for master diploma theses prepared by the urban planning students of the Faculty of Architecture at RWTH. As a result, 15 diploma proposals for the new university were presented in February 2005 to the Omani partners by the Rector jointly with the supervisors Prof. Jansen and Prof. Westerheide.

The studies and several ideas worked out by the Jansen team were later included in the final master plan designed by the new joint office of Höhler/Al Salmy, in Muscat who had been suggested by the RWTH Senate Advisor to the Omani owners and finally approved for the project.

By April 2005 a first joint draft for a Constitution was presented by the Aachen law firm Sina Maassen. It included the basic structure and rules of the future GUtech as discussed with the Omani delegation during their first official visit to Aachen. A first formulation of the *Mission* and *Vision* of the planned university was based in accordance with the ethics and philosophy of Oman and in accordance with the principles of RWTH and other German academic institutions abroad.

FIG. 28/04:
Working meeting at the Rector's Office at RWTH Aachen.
From left: His Excellency Sheikh Abdullah bin Mohammed Al Salmi, Dr. Judith
Rauhut, Prof. Dr. Burkhard Rauhut, RWTH Chancellor Dr. Michael Stückradt.

FIG. 29/05:
Working meeting at RWTH Aachen
From left: Dr. Heide Naderer, Prof. Rolf
Westerheide, Prof. Dr. Matthias Jarke,
Prof. Dr. Michael Bastian, Dr. Trautwein,
Prof. Dr. Janos Urai.

FIG. 30/05:
Signing Ceremony in the Golden
Book of Aachen
From left: Prof. Dr. Michael Jansen,
His Excellency Sheikh Abdullah
bin Mohammed Al Salmi,
Prof. Dr. Burkhard Rauhut,
Prof. Dr. Ridwan Al Sayyed.

FIG. 31/05:
Farewell.
Centre from left: His Excellency Sheikh
Abdullah bin Mohammed Al Salmi,
Prof. Dr. Burkhard Rauhut,
From right: Dr. Abdulrahman Al Salimi.

After completion of the preparatory work In October 2005 the Senate of RWTH had been again informed accordingly by the Rector about the activities in Oman and further meetings were held with the selected coordinators from the different faculties involved.

The comparative studies undertaken on German universities abroad resulted in a visit to the German University of Cairo, where in October 2005 a RWTH delegation headed by the Rector was welcomed.

Based on the pre-feasibility study and the research done so far, Al Baraka Economic Consultancy, Muscat, was asked to draw up a techno-economic Feasibility Study as a part of the final application to the Ministry of Higher Education. The revised form of the *Feasibility study for the establishment of a private university with an RWTH charter in Oman* was completed in August 2005 and at the end of the year the official application sent to the Ministry.

In March 2006 all joint efforts were finally rewarded by the Ministry of Higher Education granting a preliminary licence to establish a private university resulting in further intensive activities in all the sectors involved, both in Oman and at RWTH Aachen University.

Following suggestions by the Ministry of Higher Education the curricula had to be refined and a management structure set up along with an architectural space utilisation programme.

In Oman Oman Educational Services LLC (OES) was founded and at RWTH a liaison office was established, preliminarily named 'Oman German University of Technology' (OGTech) Office (BoG 01/2007). Under coordination of Prof. Dr. R. Schmitt, Department of Quality Control, the geologist, Dr. Ch. Hilgers, began his work for RWTH. Later Dr. B. Stäuble was recruited externally as consultant to OES in Muscat, where she lived with her family.

Based on the owners' expectations that the quality *output* of the bachelor programmes should equal that at Aachen, both partners agreed on an adequate quality *input*, resulting in a pre-university phase at foundation year level to equalise the input quality for all students, primarily dealing with English language skills, natural science and other specific courses. Obligatory for all students,

technical drawing and design were introduced to promote creativity, headed by Heiner Hoffmann, Professor emeritus of RWTH. Dr. Günter Flügge, Professor emeritus of Physics at RWTH Aachen, was appointed as initial coordinator of the Foundation Course which was started in autumn 2007 to allow the first Bachelor programme to begin in autumn 2008.

This event has allowed GUtech to celebrate the year 2017 as the 10th anniversary!

The Aachen law firm Sina Maassen was contracted to draw up the University Constitution (*Collaborative Agreement,* CA). Other constitutions were carefully studied. In the draft constitution Oman Educational Services LLC (OES) assigned overall responsibility. A Board of Directors and a Board of Governors were established to manage what would later become GUtech. While the Board of Governors, which currently meets twice a year, primarily advises the Board of Directors, it is also responsible for controlling GUtech, while the Board of Directors has the final say in approving the annual plans.

Regarding the search for suitable staff for the future management structure it was decided to appoint:

1. Coordinating professors at RWTH for each of the faculties to be set up
2. Members of the teaching staff at RWTH for the future Rectorate
3. Experts with international experience in the related field as teaching staff
4. An infrastructure at RWTH as future liaison office between the 'mother' and 'daughter' universities.

In October 2005 a first curricular programme for the four faculties had already been designed in cooperation with the Rectorate and the Jansen team as part of the application to the Ministry of Higher Education. The newly appointed scientific coordinators from RWTH, later to become the inaugural deans for the four facul-

FIG. 32/05:
Reception by the Deputy Mayor of Aachen Mrs Astrid Ströbele at the Town Hall of Aachen on the occasion of the visit of His Excellency Sheikh Abdullah bin Mohammed Al Salmi.

FIG. 33/06:
Working Meeting at the Rector's office of RWTH.
From right: Chancellor Manfred Nettekoven,
Prof. Dr. Burkhard Rauhut, Prof. Dr. Janos Urai.

ties, Prof. Fromhold-Eisebith, Prof. M. Jarke, Prof. J. Urai, and Prof. R. Westerheide, added the final touches to the curricula in 2006 together with the GUtech team.

Finally, on December 26th 2006 the *Collaborative Agreement* between OES and RWTH was signed in the presence of Her Excellency Dr. Rawya bint Saud Al Busaidi, Minister of Higher Education, by His Excellency Sheikh Abdullah bin Salim Al Salmi and Prof. Dr. Burkhard Rauhut, Rector of RWTH Aachen University. Amongst the many honourable guests were Prof. Hans Küng, the German Ambassador HE Klaus Geyer, the Inaugural Deans, the Lord Mayor of Aachen, Dr. Jürgen Linden and the RWTH team involved.

2007

In accordance with the *Collaborative Agreement*, the first Board of Governors meeting was held at RWTH Aachen on February 9th 2007 under the chairmanship of the Rector, Prof. B. Rauhut, with His Excellency Sheikh Abdullah bin Salim Al Salmi, CEO of OES, and Prof. M. Jansen as active members. Observers were Mr Nettekoven (Head of Administration), Dr. Stäuble, Dr. Hilgers, and Mr Wenhold.

At this first meeting (Resolution 08–01/2007) Prof. Jansen was appointed as Acting Rector, Dr. Hilgers as Vice-Rector, Dr. Stäuble as Academic Director and Mr Wenhold, assistant at the Machine Tool Laboratory (Werkzeugmaschinenlabor, WZL) at RWTH as Secretary. Dr. Hilgers and Dr. Stäuble were asked to take care of operations at the later GUtech.

At this board meeting the *Vision*, *Mission* and *Values* were approved as follows:

VISION:
OGtech will strive to become the leading University of Technology in the region, thus defining the highest standards in teaching and research.

MISSION:
OGtech is dedicated to educating students as highly qualified and responsibly-minded graduates in accordance with German standards, with a firm grounding in their Omani heritage. The University fosters creative and critical thinking in the advancement of research and development, resulting in benefits to society, industry and the region.

VALUES:
OGtech is committed to a non-discriminatory culture that welcomes people of any gender, and from all ethnic, geographical and racial backgrounds. The University promotes ethical principles, and encourages a culture of tolerance and harmony.

These goals had already been emphasized in speeches by the owners in May 2005 at RWTH and in Aachen cathedral, summarized in a book by His Excellency Sheikh Abdullah bin Mohammed Al Salmi published in 2016 by Olms Publisher, Germany. In March 2007 all joint efforts were again recognised by the Ministry of Higher Education (MoHE) as the final licence establishing the private university was issued, although some conditions still had to be fulfilled: Article 3 of the Decision mentioned: 'The founders shall be granted a six month period, effective from the date this decision shall come into force, to complete the procedures necessary for the University to practise its business, and a decision by the Minister of High Education shall be issued for the commencement of study in the University'.

After satisfactory approval by the MoHE for the University to practice its business, in August 2007 the final approval was given for the four programmes:

1. Bachelor of Science in Applied Geosciences
2. Bachelor of Science in Regional Management and Tourism
3. Bachelor of Science in Urban Planning and Architectural Design
4. Bachelor of Science in Applied Information Technology

FIG. 34/06:
26.12.2006 Signing of Agreement between OES and RWTH Aachen. From left: the German Ambassador His Excellency Klaus Geyer, the Rector of RWTH Aachen Prof. Dr. Burkhard Rauhut, the Minister of Higher Education Her Excellency Dr. Rawya bint Saud Al Busaidi.

FIG. 35/06:
During the signing Ceremony from left: Prof. Dr. Burkhard Rauhut, Her Excellency Dr. Rawya bint Saud Al Busaidi, His Excellency Sheikh Abdullah bin Salim Al Salmi.

FIG. 36/06:
During the Signing Ceremony from left: RWTH Chancellor Manfred Nettekoven, Prof. Dr. Hans Küng, His Excellency Sheikh Abdullah bin Mohammed Al Salmi.

In addition, initial preparatory courses commenced in the Foundation Year in autumn 2007 to allow the current Bachelor programmes to start in autumn 2008.

Based on this approval the year 2007 has been identified as the official start of teaching at GUtech.

The employment of staff, selected by the Acting Rectors team in Muscat, took place on two levels:

1. Employment at local level of administrative staff to run the university, such as IT experts, secretaries, technicians, a librarian, economists,
2. The employment of teachers and academics. Prof. Dr. Flügge was appointed by the Rector of RWTH as Head of the Foundation Course; Mr Harrison was engaged for English, Prof. Heiner Hoffmann, Emeritus Professor of Applied Art, RWTH, agreed to take on technical drawing and creative design.

In June 2007 a contract with the Goethe-Institute was signed to join the campus.

Upon request of the owners and in agreement with the *Collaborative Agreement* (2.1.4.5) the responsibility for the execution of the architecture programme had also been placed in the hands of Prof. Jansen and his team. First inspirations for a master plan had already been gathered from the previous preparatory studies and the master theses presented in February 2005 at the Faculty of Architecture RWTH.

In view of the pressure to start the Foundation courses in autumn 2007 and of the practical constraints resulting from the fact that a suitable site had not yet been identified and allocated by the Government for the university buildings, an interim solution had to be found.

With the help of the Muscat architects Al Jazira, and following the examination of a number of sites potentially able to accommodate the Foundation course, the administration and also the first

Bachelor programmes already planned for the end of 2008, two villas (later given the name Beach Campus) consisting of four house units were selected in Al Athaiba, situated both close to the sea and within easy reach of the city. The land around the villas offered enough space for temporary portakabins. From July 2007 onwards the portakabins were set up and on 6th October the first 60 students were welcomed to the initial Orientation Day.

The Beach Campus served its purpose for more than four years before it was decided to move to a larger compound, soon known as the 'Airport Campus' due to its proximity to the new airport.

Meanwhile, amongst other offers, the Government had granted 500,000 sqm of land near the village of Halban where in 2012 building began on the present campus under the supervision of Hoehler + Partner (H+P). Within a record time of 20 months! the Halban Campus could be completed.

Due to their personal engagement with the Department of Urban History, RWTH, since 2004 the architects Muhammad bin Sultan Al Salmyand Ernst Höhler had already been advising the coordinating team at the Department of Urban History, RWTH, in architectural and planning questions.

Based on the pre-requisite that the architects of the future university should be RWTH alumni, the studio Hoehler + Partner (H+P), Aachen had consequently been commissioned to prepare the final master plan and the detailed design for the main GUtech building. For this, they joined forces with the architect's office Al Jazira, Sultan and Muhammad bin Sultan Al Salmy, Muscat.

OTHER ACTIVITIES:
From July 11th–13th 2007 the later GUtech was presented in Berlin to the German Arab Business Forum, headed by Dr. Thomas Bach, who, being already familiar with RWTH, welcomed their activities in Oman. On October 21st 2007 the Acting Rector was invited by the Research Council to participate in the first Conference on Research Strategies in Oman. As a result, he was appointed member

FIG. 37/07:
The 'Beach Villas', first accomodation for GUtech.

FIG. 38/07:
Fisher Boats in front of the 'Beach Villas'.

FIG. 39/07: Above:
Prof. Dr. Robert Schmitt and Prof. Dr. Barbara Stäuble in the entrance lobby of the 'Beach Villas'.

FIG. 40/07: Above left:
First GUtech (then OGtech) Team in the premises of the Beach Villa.
From left above: Prof. Dr. Christoph Hilgers, IT-Expert Jiji Tom, Architect Muhammad bin Sultan Al Salmy, His Excellency Sheikh Abdullah bin Salim Al Salmi, Prof. Dr. Günter Flügge, Prof. Dr. Michael Jansen, Architect Ernst Höhler
Form left below: Prof. Dr. Barbara Stäuble with Hasna Al Balushi, Fatima El Madkouri, Sousann El Faksch.

FIG. 41/07: Below left:
From left: Prof. Dr. Burkhard Rauhut, then Rector of RWTH Aachen and Prof. Dr. Michael Jansen, Founding Rector of GUtech (then OGtech).

FIG. 42/08:
Prof. Heiner Hoffmann, RWTH
Aachen, teaching Design in the
Foundation Year.

FIG. 43/08:
Group photo of GUtech delegation with RWTH representatives
in the RWTH main building.

of the Executive Board of the Strategic Implementation Team (SIT) for the Science and Technology Valley Project for which the Aachen coordination team developed a first master plan on a site close to the Sultan Qaboos University. There would be opportunities to host the GUtech university within the SIT programme.

After having attended the Arab-German Business Forum in Berlin in July 2007 and the iMOVE conference in October in Berlin, the Acting Rector was invited to participate in the meeting of the German Economic Delegation to the Sultanate of Oman at the 10th session of the German-Omani Joint Commission on Economic and Technical Co-operation in Muscat from October 22nd–23rd 2007.

A major result of this meeting was the registration of the university within the bilateral agreement on economic and technical co-operation. On the occasion of the visit of the trade delegation to the Beach Campus, presents of swords and khanjars were given to Dr. Bernd Pfaffenbach, Secretary of State at the Federal Ministry of Economics and Technology and his two colleagues Mr Antonius Denz and Dr. Jürgen Friedrich, to Klaus Geyer, the German Ambassador, and to Mrs Sabine Gummersbach-Majoroh of the iMOVE Federal Institute of Vocational Training.

2008

After the successful start of the Foundation Course, the year 2008 had to be dedicated to finalizing the teaching programme for the first four Bachelor courses of Applied Geology, Architecture and Urban Planning, IT, and Tourism.

At the end of March 2008 another high-ranking delegation visited Muscat and the Beach Campus, headed by the Secretary of State for Education and Training, Andreas Storm.

Discussions were held with the delegates on cooperation in the field of technical and vocational education and the training of life-long learning concepts.

On April 23rd 2008 a strategic workshop was held in Aachen at the invitation of the Rector of RWTH to discuss quality management and to define the education profile for the first Bachelor courses. During this workshop the Acting Rector of GUtech presented the various proposals for the future university building. One offer of land by the Ministry of Housing was a compound of approximately 500,000 sqm, situated near to the sea to the east of Quriat but a long way away from the city of Muscat. Finally, the second offer, the Halban site, was accepted by the owners.

On September 1st 2008 the duties of RWTH Prof. M. Jansen as Founding and Acting Rector of GUtech were completed, also due to his further teaching obligations and to Prof. B. Rauhut taking over his position as Rector of GUtech. One of Prof. Rauhut's first actions was the welcoming of the initial batch of students for the first Bachelor year at the GUtech Beach Campus.

Our special thanks go to my team members at the Department of History of Urbanization at the Faculty of Architecture of RWTH Aachen University. To mention ahead is Dr. Karsten Ley (now professor) as the coordinator of the activities and especially involved with the feasibility studies, the original curricula and the collaboration with the administration and inaugurating deans of the new faculties at GUtech. Further to mention is Dipl.-Ing. Geesche Beth for her tireless engagement in elaborating the architectural space programmes. Finally, Muhammad bin Sultan Al Salmy B. Arch., who became researcher in our department in 2004. The latter was essentially involved in the data collection for the feasibility studies and the set-up of the Beach Campus, also serving as liaison to the Omani owner family. Later he became partner of Höhler & alSalmy, who were contracted to build the new university.

The joint efforts were honoured on June 20th 2006 with the letter of the 'Tentative Agreement'.

FIG. 44/08:
Prof. Michael Jansen teaching history of urbanization to the very first batch of UPAD (Urban Planning and Architectural Design) students.

FIG. 45/08:
Classrooms in portakabins behind the villas.

FIG. 46/15:
Visit to Oman and GUtech by the (then) Bishop of Aachen
Dr. Heinrich Mussinghoff and the Provost of Aachen Cathedral,
Manfred von Holtum.

FIG. 47/07:
Ruin of a historic mud brick
building in Bowshar, Muscat.

FIG. 48/08:
National Day Celebration 2009 with Rector Prof.
Dr. Burkhard Rauhut, Dr. Judith Rauhut and their
team in front of the "Beach Villas" in Al Athaiba.

CHAPTER 3
THE BEGINNING

THE GROWTH PHASE PRECEDING THE HALBAN CAMPUS

Prof. Dr. Dr. Burkhard Rauhut, Rector of GUtech 2008–2013

ACADEMIC DEVELOPMENT

A brand new university usually passes through several phases until it is visible on the academic landscape.

The whole process starts with the vision and the will of an individual, an institution or a government to establish a new university, followed by the overcoming of bureaucratic hurdles and culminating in the formal founding act. At this point the decision concerning the location and the building will have already been made.

The last step before the first students can enter the new university is the appointment of the necessary administrative and academic staff.

These first phases in the establishment of GUtech were described in the previous chapter by Prof. Dr. Michael Jansen, who was appointed by the Board of Directors as Acting Rector of GUtech in addition to his position as Professor of Urban History at RWTH Aachen University (RWTH). His term at GUtech ended in August 2008 and he was succeeded in September 2008 by Prof. Dr. Burkhard Rauhut, who had completed his last term as Rector of RWTH in July 2008.

At this time the number of students who had been enrolled in 2007 had declined from 60 to 58, 14 of them participating in an Intensive English programme and 44 in the Pre-University programme. For this small group of students 11 academic and 13 administrative staff were responsible. Bachelor programmes could not start initially, because high school graduates from the region were not properly prepared to start on a regular university programme due to their deficiencies in skills such as languages, mathematics and other areas.

Compared with well-established universities the number of students GUtech started with appears to be very small. However, the reasons for this situation are quite obvious: GUtech was brand new, nobody knew anything about the quality. Moreover, the government-financed Sultan Qaboos University offered places at the university for Omani students free of charge whereas GUtech had to ask relatively high tuition fees. Additionally, since people noticed that 'German' is part of the university name, many of them thought that the language of instruction would be German too—in fact it is English.

In order to increase the number of student applicants GUtech initiated a variety of activities such as advertising campaigns in newspapers, visits to schools, and participation in education fairs. As a result, the number of students enrolled at GUtech at the beginning of the Winter Term 2008/2009 reached 135, taught and administered by 28 academics and 21 administrators.

One of the main goals of GUtech was—and still is—ensuring the high quality of all its activities, including the quality of the study programmes and teaching performance. It was therefore part of the Collaborative Agreement (CA) with RWTH that for each programme offered by GUtech one professor from Aachen should act as an Inaugural Dean supervising programme and teaching performance until the first graduates could leave GUtech in 2012. The following professors from RWTH agreed to act as Inaugural Deans:

Prof. Dr. Matthias Jarke
Applied Information Technology

Prof. Dr. Janos Urai
Applied Geosciences

Prof. Rolf Westerheide
Urban Planning and Architectural Design

Prof. Dr. Martina Fromhold-Eisebith
Regional Management and Tourism

FIG. 49/08:
School children during
briefing at GUtech.

FIG. 50/09:
Prof. Dr. Matthias Jarke
with students.

FIG. 51/12:
The first batch of UPAD Students (Urban Planning and Architectural Design) during the graduation ceremony 2012.

Moreover, Prof. Dr. Günter Flügge from RWTH Aachen University was appointed as coordinator for the Pre-University programme.

Besides the supervision from Aachen University the German Accreditation Company ACQUIN (Akkreditierungs-, Certifizierungs- und Qualitätssicherungs-Institut) evaluated the four eight-semester Bachelor programmes GUtech offered. After two visits to RWTH in March 2008 and to GUtech in January 2009 all Bachelor programmes and the Pre-University programme were accredited. This was the first time that study programmes in Oman had received international accreditation!

The quality standards set by GUtech meant that only 25 out of the students who entered the Intensive English or the Pre-University programmes at GUtech in 2007 succeeded in entering the initial Bachelor programme in one of the above-mentioned subjects. Of the 94 new students entering GUtech in autumn 2008 only 9 were accepted directly for one of the Bachelor programmes. The remainder of the students were allocated either to the Intensive English or the Pre-University programme depending on the outcome of the tests they had to complete.

Due to the fact that only 34 students were enrolled in the four Bachelor programmes, 82 % of them women, the teaching staff for these programmes comprised only 10 people whereas 18 academics served in the non-Bachelor programmes. However, with the increasing number of students in the following years the proportion of students to faculty changed. In the academic year 2012/13 a total of 619 students were taught by 71 academics.

In addition to the academic staff employed by GUtech a number of fly-in teachers, mainly professors from RWTH, provide special courses within the various Bachelor programmes. On average, around 20 % of the course programme is covered by fly-ins.

Students entering a brand-new university possess only theoretical knowledge about the differences in personal responsibility, behaviour and kind of teaching and learning at a university compared with their high school experiences. Usually advanced students at well-established universities tell the freshmen about life at the university — but a new university has no advanced students. Therefore GUtech asked advanced students from RWTH to spend one or two semesters at GUtech to pass on their experience. Moreover, they assisted GUtech's faculty in tutorials and led student learner groups. In addition, a student exchange programme was signed with different German universities.

In 2007 GUtech started with an Intensive English programme and a Pre-University (Foundation Year) programme. The four Bachelor programmes which were specified in the Collaborative Agreement between Oman Educational Services LLC (OES) and RWTH on December 27th 2006 started in 2008. The experience gained in running these programmes led to some further name changes and the addition of new programmes. Applied Information Technology (IT) was narrowed down to IT for Business and Management and later on to IT for Business and Engineering; Regional Management and Tourism became Sustainable Tourism and Regional Development, and in 2012 GUtech won the approval of the Ministry of Higher Education (MoHE) to change the official name from Applied IT to Computer Science.

In 2010 two new Bachelor programmes were approved by MoHE: BSc in Mechanical Engineering and BSc in Process Engineering. Moreover, an executive Master programme in Petroleum Geosciences was approved by MoHE and in all these programmes students were enrolled for the academic year 2010/2011. The proposal by GUtech to introduce a Bachelor programme in Civil Engineering (Water Management) was rejected but another new programme, Environmental Engineering was approved for the academic year 2012/2013.

The academic structure of GUtech was established in line with the modifications to the study programmes. Based on the specifications in the CA the structure in 2013 was as follows:

FIG. 52/07:
The "Beach Villas"
in Al Athaiba.

FIG. 53/09:
The Accreditation Team of
ACQUIN Germany, in front of
the "Beach Villas" in 2009.

FIG. 55/10:
The new 'Airport' Campus near the Sultan Qaboos Highway.

FIG. 54/10:
The decoration of the building during the 40th National Day Celebration in 2010.

FIG. 56/10:
The 'Ribbon Cutting Ceremony' by Her Excellency Dr. Rawya bint Saud Al Busaidi together with the German Ambassador Her Excellency Angelika Storz-Chakarji, and Prof. Dr. Ernst Schmachtenberg, Rector of RWTH Aachen University.

Pre-University Unit:
- *Intensive English Programme*

- *Foundation Year Programme*

Faculty of Sciences
- *Mathematics and Science (Support)*

- *Applied Geosciences (BSc)*

- *Petroleum Geosciences (MSc)*

Faculty of Urban Planning and Architectural Design
- *Urban Planning and Architectural Design (BSc)*

Faculty of Engineering
- *Computer Science (BSc)*

- *Mechanical Engineering (BEng)*

- *Process Engineering (BEng)*

- *Environmental Engineering (BEng)*

Faculty of Business and Management
- *Sustainable Tourism and Regional Development (BSc)*

In 2008 the first 34 students had commenced the four Bachelor programmes GUtech had started with. In the first graduation ceremo-ny held at GUtech on December 8th 2012 thirty of them received their certificates after successfully completing their studies. One of the graduates in Geosciences, Kawther Al Quraishi, described her experience at GUtech in the following way:

'It is a tough university, where you really need to work a lot, but the pressure makes the diamond'.

GOVERNANCE DEVELOPMENT
The main principles of the governance of GUtech are pre-assigned in the Collaborative Agreement. In short, the CA allocates academic responsibility to RWTH and financial responsibility to OES. This is reflected in the fact that the Board of Directors (BoD) has budgetary sovereignty. The BoD comprises the owners of OES (and one representative from RWTH) whereas the Board of Governors (BoG) decides on academic issues at GUtech and is chaired by the Rector of RWTH. Moreover, the majority in the BoG is on the German side.

When the Bachelor programmes started in October 2008 many academic guidelines had already been passed by the BoG, such as Academic Regulations, Recruitment Policy, the Constitution and the change of name from OGTech to GUtech. Additionally, the management team in the academic year 2007/2008 — Acting Rector Prof. Dr. Michael Jansen, Deputy Rector Prof. Dr. Christoph Hilgers and Academic Director Prof. Barbara Stäuble — had prepared a Business Plan for the period 2007–2017.

In 2009 the so-called University Council was replaced by the Rectorate comprising the Rector Prof. Rauhut, the Deputy Rector for Academic Affairs Prof. Dr. Stäuble and a Deputy Rector for Administration and Finances, with Dr. Hussain Al Salmi replacing Prof. Dr. Hilgers. Also in 2009 the first Student Council was elected.

The CA calls the time from beginning of the Bachelor programmes until the first graduation the Initial Period. After the Initial Period the Inaugural Deans from RWTH were replaced by Deans elected by the staff of the respective faculties at GUtech, and Department

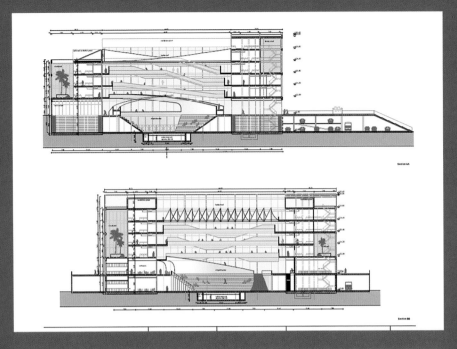

FIG. 57/10:
Architectural plans showing the cross section of the Halban plan with the inner courtyard.

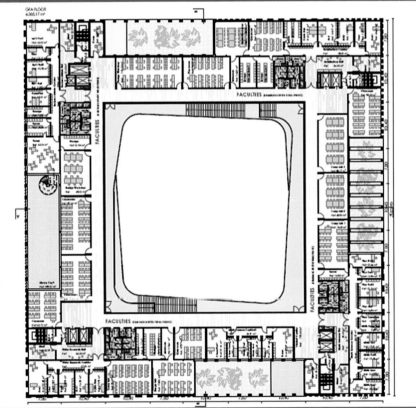

FIG. 58/10:
Ground plan of the university with central courtyard in form of an 'arena'.

FIG 59/12:
The Halban Campus was
built within 20 months
in 2012 and 2013.

FIG. 60/12:
The honouring of the
labourers and technicians
during the topping out
ceremony. The construction
took place without any
accident.

Boards, Faculty Boards and the Academic Board were established. Prof. Dr. Barbara Stäuble, who was at first Project Manager in 2007, then Academic Director until 2009 before she was promoted to Deputy Rector for Academic Affairs, left GUtech in July 2012 and was replaced by Dr. Jürgen Werner.

Good governance is always based on reliable information, its availability and on an effective process to promptly update it. Thanks to a four-year grant from the German Academic Exchange Service (DAAD), the Machine Tool Laboratory WZL at RWTH, headed by Prof. Dr. Robert Schmitt, was able to develop a Quality Management System, a software named QWicki, which supplemented the Enterprise Resource Planning System (ERP) that had been implemented at GUtech in 2010.

PREMISES DEVELOPMENT

OGTech started its activities in two rented villas close to the beach in Al Athaiba, Muscat. Originally the buildings were ordinary houses, which then had to be converted into university buildings, though they offered only around 400 sqm of space. Some portakabins were therefore added, thus creating enough space to accommodate the first sixty students together with faculty and administration. These premises were named Beach Campus (BC).

Since the number of students had reached 135 in 2009 two more portakabins were erected, increasing the capacity to 200 students. In anticipation of more students in the coming year, in April 2010 an interim solution was found, after a very intensive search, in the form of the purchase of a newly erected nine-storey building situated directly next to the Sultan Qaboos Highway and close to Muscat International Airport. The immediate proximity to the Airport and the highway transformed this building into a landmark and made GUtech visible to anyone passing by. It was named Airport Campus (AC) when GUtech moved there in October 2010.

The building was totally empty, without inner walls, and had to be converted into a building capable of accommodating a university, with offices, lecture rooms, laboratories, a canteen and an IT infrastructure. Since AC was still too small, GUtech separated the pre-university activities taking place at BC from the Bachelor education offered at AC. Additionally, GUtech rented several villas in Al Athaiba close to BC to host fly-in professors and interns. The villas were also used to provide office space for some of the GUtech scientists.

Both BC and AC were interim 'homes' for GUtech. The final campus was planned at Halban, around 35 km from Muscat Airport, on a 500,000 sqm piece of land granted by His Majesty Sultan Qaboos bin Said Al Said in 2007.

Firstly, the Faculty of Architecture at RWTH organised an architecture competition to create ideas for a master plan. Finally, the architecture office Höhler+Partner LLC, a newly established architecture office with both Omani and German partners, was awarded the contract for developing a master plan. This plan proposed the erection, in an initial phase, of the Main Building of the university with around 20,000 sqm usable space with capacity for 2000 students, student housing for around 200 students and a Museum of Islamic Sciences.

The plan was first presented to the BoG in December 2009, the call for tenders started in October 2010, a ground-breaking ceremony took place in February 2011, the topping-out ceremony was organised in January 2012 and GUtech relocated to the so-called Halban Campus (HC) in September 2012—an outstanding construction achievement, with the Main Building and the housing being completed within only 18 months. Moreover, the Main Building has been recognised internationally in the form of the German Design Council's Design Award 2016 in the category Excellent Communications Design—Architecture.

MISCELLANEOUS

Universities compete with each other for students, for academic and administrative staff, for research grants, for financial support and

FIG. 61/12:
Prof. Dr. Burkhard Rauhut addressing the audience in the Airport Campus during the Engineering Conference 2012. First row from left: Prof. Dr. Barbara Stäuble, Prof. Dr. Michael Modigell, Dr. Hussain Al Salmi, Rector of RWTH Prof. Dr. Ernst Schmachtenberg.

FIG. 62/12:
GUtech Workshop at RWTH Aachen University with members of the Board of Governors and the German Ambassador to Oman Her Excellency Angelika Storz-Chakarji in June 2012

FIG. 63/12:
The Mathematics Conference 2012 in the Airport Campus, organized by Prof. Bernhard Heim and attended by (from left) Prof. Dr. Barbara Stäuble, the German Ambassador to Oman Her Excellency Angelika Storz-Chakarji, GUtech Rector Prof. Dr. Burkhard Rauhut and various guests from Oman.

for student scholarships. This is extremely important—and difficult—for a brand-new university starting from scratch like GUtech.

Immediately after the signing of the Collaborative Agreement the new university was advertised in Omani newspapers, on the university website and by the Acting Rector Prof. Jansen at the various conferences he attended. At the German-Oman Meeting on Economy in Muscat in October 2007 GUtech was registered within the framework of the bilateral agreement on economic and technical co-operation between the two countries.

In order to promote the new university, academics and marketing experts from GUtech gave lectures at various secondary/high schools, attended education fairs in the region and organised meetings with representatives from industry to disseminate the message about the new university of technology with German roots but with English as language of teaching. In order to raise awareness of the importance of science, and to attract the parents of prospective students, GUtech organised regular Public Lectures given by researchers from GUtech or by invited speakers. Also hosted by GUtech were international conferences such as two Engineering Conferences in January 2012 and February 2013, and an International Mathematics Workshop in February 2012.

Though Germany does not finance GUtech the respective German Ambassadors—His Excellency Klaus Geyer 2006–2009, Her Excellency Angelika Storz-Chakarji 2009–2012 and His Excellency Hans-Christian von Reibnitz since 2012—have helped to guide GUtech as members of the BoG and have used their contacts in Oman to promote the university. They have also brought German delegations from industry and politics to visit GUtech hoping to thus generate support for the university, though mostly in vain. However, the decision of RWTH to award GUtech the status of an AN-Institut of RWTH was very helpful: staff and students of GUtech were granted free access to RWTH's electronic library.

Very beneficial to the reputation of GUtech were the visits of top-ranking German politicians like the Federal Health Minister His Excellency Dr. Philipp Rösler in January 2011, the Federal Minister for Foreign Affairs His Excellency Dr. Guido Westerwelle in May 2011, the Federal President of Germany His Excellency Dr. Christian Wulff in December 2011 and the President of the German Parliament Norbert Lammert in March 2013.

With regard to GUtech's reputation in Oman, the most important visit by far was the visit of His Majesty Sultan Qaboos bin Said Al Said on December 24th 2012. This recognition by His Majesty cannot be over-emphasized as GUtech was the first private university in Oman he has ever visited. Accordingly, 24th of December has been approved as a GUtech annual holiday named University Day.

Activities at a university are not limited to teaching and research. Extracurricular activities of staff and students are important ingredients in the quality of life at the university. They are a kind of soft factor in the decision of prospective students to join a specific university. In this respect GUtech offers many leisure opportunities for staff and students, such as membership in various clubs like the Robotics Club or the IT Club, outdoor activities like canoeing or sailing courses or desert trekking, and a variety of sport offers for men and women alike, such as like football, futsal, basketball, riding, table tennis, aerobics, zumba and yoga.

Of special importance was the participation of staff and students from the Architecture Department of GUtech in the Eco-House Design Competition organised by The Research Council of Oman (TRC) in 2011. The goal was the design and construction of an eco-friendly house with respect to energy consumption, adapted to the environment in Oman. Five universities and colleges took part in the competition, which consisted of eight individually-scored contests. GUtech came top in four of these contests (Conceptual Design and Development, Architecture, Communications, and Comfort Zone) and was awarded second place overall.

In April 2013 Prof. Dr. Michael Modigell replaced Prof. Dr. Burkhard Rauhut as Rector of GUtech.

CHAPTER 4
THE CONSOLIDATION

THE CONSOLIDATION PHASE

Prof. Dr. Michael Modigell, Rector of GUtech 2013–2020

As already mentioned in the previous chapter the numbers of new students started to increase dramatically in the academic year 2012/13. This was caused by the decision of the government to provide financial support for all students in higher education and to allow as many young people as possible to get a higher education. This resulted in a significant increase in the number of new students at all institutions of higher education, not only at GUtech. Between the academic years 2011/12 and 2013/14 the number of students more than doubled. This trend continued; it was almost a numbers explosion. By 2014 GUtech already had 1100 students — compared with 370 in 2011.

In 2017/18, GUtech had 1964 students: 725 in the Foundation year and 1239 on the Bachelor programmes. 85% of the students are Omani and 15% are from other countries, with the majority being the children of expatriate families. Only 4 students are truly international, that is they came to Oman primarily to study.

The students are taught by 70 faculty, 38 of them on the Foundation programme, GUbridge. Four of the faculty on the Bachelor programmes are Full Professors, 7 are Associate Professors, 12 Assistant Professors, and 9 are Lecturers.

Corresponding to this general development the number of students on the different programmes has grown continuously, except for the programmes in Computer Science and Sustainable Tourism and Regional Development. Contrary to expectations, here the number of students has been low and has not grown significantly. On the Tourism programme the numbers actually decreased, even though the tourism industry has been nominated as one of Oman's future key industries. In 2014 the Tourism programme was carefully revised and adjusted to include more general management aspects; it was then renamed International Business and Service Management. It started in 2015 and was successful from the beginning. The Computer Science Department made special efforts to advertise the programme and within two years the number of students doubled. It has certainly also helped that the Computer Science students are very successful in local and international competitions, and the public has become well aware of this. In 2013 a new Logistics programme was designed with the support of the Inaugural Dean of the Faculty of Business and Administration, Prof. Lorz from RWTH Aachen University. It started in 2014 and has proved successful in increasing student numbers on the International Business and Service Industries programme.

Especially successful in terms of student numbers are the Engineering programmes. Two years after launching the programmes the Engineering Department was already the strongest group within the Bachelor programmes, and it currently hosts more than 40% of the Bachelor students.

The Master programme Petroleum Geoscience did not achieve a sufficiently high status to be financially successful and will be now transferred to a new Master programme which will allow specialisation in Petroleum Geology, Hydrogeology, and Mineral Resources. The programme is in the final stage of the Ministry of Higher Education approval process and will start in 2018.

In 2015 the Engineering programmes were accredited by ACQUIN and the other Bachelor programmes were re-accredited.

In 2017 the current structure of the GUtech (with number of students and names of the Deans) was as follows:

Faculty of Science (Prof. Dr. Bernhard Heim) — Mathematics and Natural Sciences
· Applied Geoscience (230)

Faculty of Urban Planning and Architecture
(Prof. Alexander Kader)
· Urban Planning and Architectural Design (184)

Faculty of Engineering
(Assoc. Prof. Dr. Najah Al Mhanna)
· Computer Science (78)

· Mechanical Engineering (125)

· Process Engineering (228)

· Environmental Engineering (175)

Faculty of Business and Management
(Inaugural Dean Prof. Dr. Oliver Lorz)
· Logistics (172)

· International Business and Service Management (126)

Considering the turbulent development of GUtech the question arises as to its future over the next five years. Unlimited growth is unlikely due to limited resources. A few simple considerations regarding existing constraints can throw some light on this. The capacity of the Halban Campus is around 2200 students. Assuming stable conditions, meaning no change in the total number of students or the relation between the pre-university and the academic programmes, this corresponds to a flux in student numbers of 400 each year. Around 1600 students will then be participating in the academic programmes and 530 at the pre-university level. These figures can be compared with the maximum capacity of each programme within each of the faculties currently involved in the programmes. Taking into account specific limiting conditions for each programme, such as the capacity of the labs or the provision of rea-

sonably sized studios for the architects it can be shown that the theoretical capacity of the programmes corresponds to the estimated number of 400 students (+/-) each year. Based on this a detailed model of GUtech was set up which allows the university to be run in an optimal way regarding finances and the utilisation of all its resources. It seems that GUtech will achieve this status in 2018.

What will be the future development of GUtech? GUtech aims to become a university providing all levels of academic education. Consequently all departments have designed Master programmes with the support of the corresponding Chairs at RWTH Aachen University. The proposals are at different stages in the approval process at the Ministry for Higher Education. Programmes in Geoscience, Urban Planning and Architecture and Computer Science have been recently approved. The Master programmes for Engineering and MBA are still in the process. Additionally GUtech applied for a PhD programme which is research based and comparable to the PhD education offered by German universities. Hopefully, all these programmes can start in 2018.

What can we say about the quality of GUtech's students and graduates? There are a couple of indicators that are helpful in forming an opinion. Nearly 70 % of GUtech's graduates are either employed in public or private institutions or go on to study for a Master's degree within three months of graduation. Frequently, students are awarded prizes in national and international competitions. In 2014 a group of engineering students participated for the first time in the Shell Eco Marathon held in Manila. Students had to design and build a car with low fuel consumption, and finally to run it. It was a great success that they achieved fifth place in the group for diesel-powered cars. A group of GUtech Computer Science students participated in the Imagine Cup Competition organised by Microsoft, and after winning the Regional Championship in Lebanon, the team was ranked among the top eight teams in the world in the final competition in Seattle. A group of Applied Geoscience students participated in the prestigious Imperial Barrel Award in Manama (Bahrain) and won a first and third prize out of 20 teams in different disciplines.

GUtech's students are successful in sports as well. In 2016 GUtech teams won a gold, a silver and two bronze medals in the Taekwondo Championships for Higher Educational Institutions in Oman, also winning a gold medal at the Open Female Badminton Championships in 2016. The GUtech female futsal team achieved the fourth place at a competition held in 2017.

GUtech, as part of Omani society, aims to support the community too. GUtech professors work for different ministries as advisers, for example in the development of tourism or urban planning. GUtech advises the NAHI (National Automotive Higher Institute) on creating and running an automotive training centre. GUtech supplied the Duqm programme, an initiative to improve the employability of young people of the Duqm area.

For the general public GUtech frequently organises events on campus such as charity events, the World Water Day (organised together with the Ministry of Regional Municipality), environmental events, the Poetry Gathering and others. These events are recognised by the public and attendance is significant.

ACADEMIC COOPERATION

The most important academic partner of GUtech is with certainty RWTH Aachen University because of the Affiliation Contract. This is documented in the high number of Aachen faculty who are fly-ins, or who act as advisers to the faculties, as is the case with the former Inaugural Deans and the acting Inaugural Dean, or who advise the large number of joint research projects. There is one special aspect of the cooperation, which appears to be unique, the so-called Interns. These are Master or PhD students from RWTH who spend one or two semesters at GUtech and who serve as student helpers in the corresponding departments. Around 30 students come each semester to GUtech. In principle their tasks are comparable to those of PhD students at German universities: performing ex-ercises, holding tutorials and working in the labs, advising the students on their project work and academic life, and supporting the departments in their administrative work. It has been shown that they give essential support to the academic staff and that they create a distinctly international atmosphere. Their advice to the students is of special value because the interns are still students themselves and communicate on a level acceptable to other students. To organise the process of recruiting interns and to prepare them for their stay at the GUtech in 2013 a contact office has been established at the Chair of Prof. Dr. R. Schmitt at the WZL—Prof. Dr. R. Schmitt is the representative of the Rector of RWTH Aachen University for the GCC area. This office additionally provides support for the recruitment of academic staff for the GUtech.

Since 2014 cooperation agreements have existed with the University of Brescia (UNIBS) in Italy and the Thai-German Graduate School in Bangkok. The cooperation with Italy has been especially fruitful. A group of Italian professors comes each semester to teach Material Science for engineers in three blocks and GUtech students go to UNIBS on internships or to write their Bachelor theses. In addition research in the field of engineering science is conducted jointly and GUtech faculty have acted as co-supervisors for three Italian PhD students. GUtech is now on the board of the International PhD programme which has been launched this year by UNIBS.

Close cooperation has been established with the Omani institutions of higher education. The heads of the private institutions meet at least once a year, under the aegis of the Ministry of Higher Education, to exchange experience and information. Agreements on joint research and education have been initiated with the International Maritime College Oman and the Military Technological College. GUtech students of Logistics, International Business and Service Management, and of Engineering Science make use of the labs of both institutions.

Successful cooperation also exists with Sultan Qaboos University, the only public university in Oman, and also the largest. This is documented by the international conferences and exhibitions jointly organised over the last few years.

R & D AT GUTECH

GUtech follows the Humboldtian education ideal: the holistic combination of studies and research. Consequently the foundations of GUtech are the three pillars of teaching, research and innovation. Teaching is represented by the students on the study programmes, research by the academic research in all disciplines, and innovation by applied research and consultancy. GUtech aims to be excellent in all three fields. Therefore experience in all three fields is considered during the selection process for new academic staff. All faculty members of GUtech are PhD holders and have documented their research activities with an appropriate number of publications.

It is certainly challenging to attempt to realise this idea in the environment of a young and small university. Besides their teaching duties, all staff are involved in the development of the university, and this is extremely time-consuming. Additionally, graduates, PhD students, and postdoctoral researchers, who in traditional universities contribute significantly to both research and teaching, are missing here. All in all the staff are left with little time to concentrate on research. Another important aspect to consider when trying to understand the University's specific difficulties is that research facilities of all kinds, from labs to workshops, were not available at GUtech in the early days.

Despite these difficulties GUtech staff have been active in R&D from the very beginning—either by focusing on theoretical work not requiring infrastructure or by cooperating on projects with colleagues abroad. The geoscientists have been especially active, strongly supported by their colleagues from RWTH who have been active in research and consultancy in Oman for many years. Two of GUtech's young scientists were recognised by the TRC (The National Research Council) in 2015 and 2017 respectively as outstanding researchers in Oman—in geoscience and engineering.

The number of publications and contributions to conferences of GUtech faculty has increased continuously. In 2016, 59 papers were published and GUtech members are editors for 13 scientific journals.

The summer break is traditionally the time of the most intensive research activities in GUtech academia. Most of them go abroad to take part in conferences and to visit their research partners for joint research activities. This is strongly supported by the university. In 2016, 31 conferences were visited and 33 talks given. GUtech staff organised five conferences and workshops and co-organised two further events with other universities.

The EcoHouse has been already mentioned as one of GUtech's outstanding research projects. It has to be emphasised that—in accordance with the spirit of GUtech—students have been (and still are) actively involved in developing and implementing the building programme.

Another fine example of student contribution to R&D is the biological waste water plant of GUtech, which has been partially designed by students within the framework of their project activities.

In 2016 Petroleum Development Group (PDO) and GUtech signed a contract agreeing close research cooperation in the specific areas important for PDO and covering a broad field of disciplines, from architecture to process engineering. In addition to this GUtech is member of a platform created jointly by the oil and gas industry and a number of universities. This platform is designed to enable the simple exchange of information between the partners in order to support applied research for the purposes of the industry, and so to improve the cooperation between industry and the universities.

INFRASTRUCTURE

A couple of problems have arisen in connection with the 'explosive' increase in the number of students. Where to accommodate the classes? In the Engineering programmes one batch of students exceeded one hundred and the same applied to the maths courses

FIG. 64/13:
In 2013 for the first time GUtech students participated in a German Language and Culture Course at the RWTH Aachen University Language Centre.

FIG. 65/16:
International Workshop of GUtech UPAD and RWTH Aachen Urban Design students at the Department of Urban Planning and Architectural Design at GUtech, Halban Campus in the winter term 2016/2017.

FIG. 66/13:
The visit of students of the Indian School Muscat (ISM) to GUtech, Halban Campus. First row from right: Dr. Manuela Gutberlet (PR), Prof. Dr. Najah Al Mhanna (Eng.), Prof. Dr. Ulrich Schnaut (Head of Engineering), Prof. Dr. Bas den Brok (Head of Applied Geosciences), Prof. Dr. Rudolf Fleischer (Head of Computer Sciences), Dr. Preshob (Student Counselor), Mr Deep Wilson (Vice-Principal of the Indian School Muscat) and ISM high school student counsellors.

FIG. 67/13: Right above: Second Engineering Conference at GUtech, Halban Campus in 2013.

FIG. 68/13: Right below: Prof. Dr. Michael Modigell addressing the audience.

FIG. 69/16:
GUtech UPAD and RWTH Aachen Urban Planning students
on excursion in Oman acccompanied by Prof. Alexander Kader
(centre left) in the winter term 2016/2017.

in cases where students of different programmes were taught together. The design of the building allows room sizes to be changed easily by combining two or more rooms into one. GUtech currently has two lecture rooms with a capacity of 120 students and another two with space for around 100 students. Additionally, the research hall, initially designed as a laboratory for machine development, was modified to serve as a multi-purpose room with space for about 400 seats or more than 200 tables. During this period all lecture rooms were equipped with projectors and the large lecture rooms with audio systems.

For the Engineering programmes a thermodynamics lab has been set up with around 30 standard experiments related to basic and advanced thermodynamics. For teaching and research purposes a well-equipped bio-engineering lab has been established. In separate premises, close to the main building, is a workshop for the engineers, equipped with 20 work places which are used by the students for project work.

The Geoscience Department has three different 'hardware' labs: a mineralogy lab for the preparation of samples, which is housed in a separate building, a microscopy lab with 20 light microscopes for teaching, and an XRD lab with an XRD machine donated by KHD, Germany.

The software equipment at GUtech for research and education is continuously improving. The Geoscience Department operates a 20-seat computer lab, which is equipped with professional geological simulation software, donated by Schlumberger, France. For general simulation purposes Comsol Multi-Physics is available. The Engineering Department has a simulation lab with CHEMCAD for teaching and professional applications. Another professional simulation software for energy and pipeline systems, developed and donated by PSI Germany, is available for student teaching purposes, training of industrial staff, and research.

GUBRIDGE

Similar to other universities in Oman GUtech operates a pre-university programme which has two functions: firstly to improve students' English language skills in order to fulfil the entry requirement of GUtech — IELTS 6.0 or comparable test — and secondly to prepare the students for the demands of the Bachelor programmes. Students who do not meet the language requirements of the university have to start either with an intensive English programme (General Foundation Programme) and then continue with the Advanced Foundation Programme or — if they already have sufficient English skills — start directly with the latter. The ratio between the two groups fluctuates, but in general one third of the students have to start with the General Foundation Programme. Analysis of the efficiency of the pre-university in 2014 showed that a re-design of the curricula for both programmes was necessary in order to focus clearly on the demands of the students and the Bachelor programmes. In 2015 GUbridge, the new pre-university level, was launched with an intensive programme in English, and in the Advanced Foundation a focused curriculum with English, maths, and computing and study skills. Additionally the Kaizen teaching method, which had been successfully applied in the maths lectures on the Bachelor programmes, has been introduced for the English and the maths lectures. Already one year later, in 2016, the success of the action was evident: The numbers of repeaters dropped by a factor of three and the percentage of students who passed the IELTS 6.0 increased by a factor of two.

FIG. 70/12:
The Board of Governors (BoG) in 2012 with GUtech students. Top row from left: Prof. Dr. Robert Schmitt, Dr. Christian Bode (DAAD), His Excellency Sheikh Abdullah bin Salim Al Salmi, Prof. Dr. Ernst Schmachtenberg, Prof. Dr. Burkhard Rauhut, Dr. Dorothea Rüland (DAAD), Prof. Dr. Michael Jansen, Dr. Hussain Al Salmi.

CHAPTER 5
MESSAGES

GUTECH IN OMAN – A BEST-PRACTICE EXAMPLE OF TRANSNATIONAL EDUCATION

Dr. Christian Bode, Former Secretary General of the German Academic Exchange Service DAAD; member of GUtech Board of Governors (BoG) since 2007

The German University of Technology in Oman is not only a rising star in the Omani higher education firmament but also a best-practice example of a quite recent development in the internationalisation of German universities — namely in the delivery of Transnational Education (TNE) and the founding of so-called 'German-backed universities' abroad.

Transnational Education is defined as the provision of teaching and study programmes by a 'mentor university' in another country ('offshore'), whereby this university takes the lead responsibility for the quality and the recognition of the degrees offered abroad. This type of 'export' of educational services was first introduced by Anglo-American and Australian universities, while German universities contented themselves — quite successfully — with the traditional forms of internationalisation, i.e. collaborative research projects, recruitment of international talents, student exchange programmes and so forth.

The former reluctance of German universities to embrace TNE may appear surprising given the fact that German industry has long been very strong in the export field, including capital investment, production and even research in foreign countries. One major reason for this discrepancy has been, and still is, that German higher education has no commercial orientation (which does not exclude economical imperatives); the most significant proof is the absence of tuition fees, even for international students. Education is seen in Germany not as a private commodity but as a 'public good' and as the single most important tool in the promotion of social cohesion and promotion.

Thus it was only in the late nineties of the last century — when the economic and political globalisation had gained a new dynamic and dimension — that German universities hesitantly embarked on TNE projects. They were encouraged by financial support from the German Academic Exchange Service (DAAD), who in turn had persuaded the Federal Government, namely the Foreign Office (AA) and the Ministry of Education and Research (BMBF), to invest in these international educational services in the interests of national visibility abroad, international friendship building and the professional competitiveness of our universities in a global market.

Since then a great number of smaller TNE projects have emerged and the steadily increasing number of almost 30,000 TNE students is more than trivial. Concentrating on the major projects, the German-backed universities, we can meanwhile count a dozen of them with the main focus on Africa/MENA and Asia (opening dates in brackets): The German-Kazakh University (1999), the Chinese German University at Tongji University in Shanghai, including the Sino-German College for Postgraduate Studies (CDHK, 1998) and the Sino-German College of Applied Sciences (CDHAW 2006), the German University in Cairo (2002), the German Institute of Science and Technology — TUM Asia in Singapore (2002), the German Jordanian University in Amman (GJU 2004), the German University of Technology in Oman (GUtech 2007), the Vietnamese-German University in Ho Chi Minh City (VGU 2008), the Turkish-German University in Istanbul (TDU 2008), the Berlin TU Campus in El Gouna (2012), the German-Russian Institute of Advanced Technologies in Kasan (GRIAT 2014) and the German Mongolian Institute for Resources and Technology (GMIT 2013)

Each of these institutions has its own particular founding history but all of them also have some common characteristics:

1.   The most significant of these is the fact that the German backed universities are not German owned. With the exception of the El Gouna Campus of the Technical University of Berlin, all these universities are foreign national universities under the HE law of the host country and with the accreditation of the respective national authorities. That is also true of GUtech in Muscat which has sometimes been misunderstood as a 'foreign university'. In all cases the premises are owned by the foreign (private or public) investor; the students are enrolled (only) at the host-university, which also employs the staff, delivers the degrees and bears the financial risks.

2.   The second important phenomenon is the strong voice of the German mentor university in all matters concerning the quality of the academic performance and results, including curricula, quality assessment, appointment of leading staff (Rector/President, Deans, Board of Trustees). The formal influence of the German university varies according to the national legal framework and is normally (but not always) stronger in the case of private universities like GUtech compared to state-run universities like TDU. German academic and sometimes even diplomatic staff sit on the boards, and in some (few) cases even the Rector/President is a German academic, as in the case of GUtech.

3.   In all cases there are Memoranda of Understanding or even formally ratified agreements between the two governments involved, sometimes including privileges of customs and visa regulations. On the German side it is sometimes the Foreign Office (AA), more recently the Ministry of Education and Research (BMBF), sometimes both. In some cases, where the initiative for the foundation originated from the political authorities, these agreements preceded the project (CDHK, TDU, VDU, Amman, GRIAT), whereas in the case of GUtech, due to the private, semi-institutional founding history, governmental recognition lagged behind in time, in format, and in content; so there is still room for improvement.

4.   Although the principal capital investment has to be provided by the host country—be it through state or private investor—there is in all cases substantial financial support from the German government through the DAAD. The financial contribution goes to the German mentor university and is earmarked for specific purposes. The common denominator of these specifications is the strengthening of the 'German dimension' of the project. And this German dimension usually involves German language instruction (often mandatory), in fly-in faculty from the mentor university, in quality assurance and in student exchange. In the case of GUtech the DAAD pays for a lecturer in German language studies, supports the University of Aachen in its quality assurance activities and sponsors student exchanges with Germany, mainly with RWTH Aachen University. It is highly advantageous if this exchange develops in both directions; this may require some innovative programmes, short and mid-term, to attract more German students to Oman.

5.   Key elements of the German dimension in higher education are three more characteristics: the mandatory combination ('unity') of teaching and research, the close cooperation with the employment sector, especially with industry, and a reasonable amount of student freedom, including curricular choices, self-learning processes and personal development through self-reliance. The latter is best enhanced by a period of study abroad, which is offered—sometimes even required (GJU)—on all TNE projects. In comparison to other TNE projects GUtech still has some room for improvement in both the number and the duration of overseas study opportunities for students and staff.

6.   Almost two thirds of the courses offered by German-backed universities are in the field of engineering and in economics/business studies, as in GUtech, reflecting both the demand from the host country and the reputation that German universities and industry enjoy. Unfortunately, social sciences and humanities play,

if at all, only a peripheral role. 'Unfortunately' because the most severe global challenges are caused by political, economic and religious tensions rather than by technical demands or deficits. GUtech, founded by wise sponsors of Omani roots and the global mindset, could be an outstanding platform to bridge gaps between our continents, cultures and ways of life. Maybe not a task for today and tomorrow, but a target that should be approached step by step.

7. The degree courses offered by German-backed universities are sometimes at Master level only, but most of them cover undergraduate studies as well. The courses are normally accredited by a German (or other international) accreditation agency. That means that a BA graduate of GUtech is formally eligible for admission to a related Master course at any German university, and since the German accreditation agency is itself accredited by the *European Association for Quality Assurance in Higher Education (ENQA)* this eligibility should also open the doors of all other European universities. This is a remarkable privilege, although eligibility does not guarantee admission, since the number of applicants may exceed the local capacity.

8. The above-mentioned eligibility privilege is further upgraded by the fact that the majority of the German universities meanwhile offer English-medium Master-courses, currently more than 800. That might lead to competition between GUtech's own Master courses and those of German technical universities, including the mentor university of Aachen. But firstly, competition is a driver of quality, and secondly, there is an instrument capable of mediating this potential rivalry, namely the dual degree programme (i.e. two Master degrees from GUtech and RWTH Aachen). Although this is an ambitious and costly scheme which also needs close and permanent interaction at staff level, GUtech should envisage this as a mid-term perspective—if not for all, then at least for some of its best graduate students.

9. Long-term stability is maybe the greatest challenge facing these 'hybrid' TNE institutions. Some Anglo-American-Australian institutions have been closed because of commercial failure, lack of governmental support and/or decreasing interest on the side of the mentor university, once the pioneer generation had left. The German-backed universities have all survived so far and the absence of the commercial dimension, the prevailing spirit of intercultural partnership and the continuous financial support and advice from DAAD and both governments are good pre-conditions for further success.

10. Nevertheless, budgets and buildings matter (especially if they are as excellent as the Halban Campus), but at the end of the day sustainable success depends even more on the people involved, on students, staff and leadership—on their dedication, spirit and passion. These were the driving forces which inspired the small group of founders of GUtech. This spirit cannot be bought, nor can it be ordered. It has to be permanently fuelled and renewed, especially as the founding generation is gradually replaced. It needs both emotional dedication and a business-like definition and synchronization of interests of all sides involved. These interests may change as time goes by. The ten-year anniversary of GUtech provides an excellent opportunity to undergo this exercise and thus lay the foundation for the coming decade.

Vivat, crescat, floreat!

STATEMENT ON THE 10ᵀᴴ ANNIVERSARY OF GUTECH

Prof. Dr. Margret Wintermantel, President of the German Academic Exchange Service DAAD since 2012

On behalf of the German Academic Exchange Service (DAAD), I would like to extend our warm congratulations on the 10ᵗʰ anniversary of the German University of Technology in Oman. We are honoured and proud to contribute to this admirable success story of GUtech since its foundation.

The history of the university goes back to the year 2003, when the honourable Al Salmi Family decided to establish a high-quality university of technology with the support of German expertise in education at university level. This extraordinary vision to build up a binational institution of higher education was the cornerstone of the flourishing development of GUtech and it was at the same time inspired by His Majesty Sultan Qaboos' directions to establish universities of high standard in Oman also with the support of private investors. Concerning the German know-how, RWTH Aachen University—which is one of the leading and top ranked universities of technology in Europe—was approached by the founders with the intention of transferring the highly demanded German expertise into higher education in Oman.

The cooperation with the DAAD has begun then with advising, mentoring and quality assurance as well as several provisions of funding provided by the Federal Ministry of Education and Research (BMBF) and granted to RWTH Aachen under the different funding schemes in the field of Transnational Education, starting in 2007 up to now. Under the umbrella of these programmes, the German universities, in collaboration with local partners, offer their study programmes abroad and so transnational education, the German dimension, quality assurance and mobility are enhanced. In addition, RWTH Aachen receives funding for scholarship offers from the Federal Foreign Office (AA).

The long tradition of the joint academic dialogue between Germany and Oman and the close cooperation between the GUtech and the DAAD is outstanding. Since its very beginnings, the GUtech has achieved much more than we dared to dream 10 years ago when the project started. Almost 2.000 students are currently enrolled in 9 different study programmes at Bachelor and Master level; during the past years, approximately 400 students have successfully graduated from this university. Within the Bachelor programmes, around 35 % of the academic staff are German. Furthermore, GUtech was the first private university in the Sultanate Oman and on the Arabian Peninsula to receive international accreditation for all its Bachelor of Science programmes by the Accreditation, Certification and Quality Assurance Institute ACQUIN in June 2009. This international accreditation is an important assurance that the GUtech students are receiving a world-class higher education in Oman. At the same time, the graduates also have the possibility to continue their studies, for example at RWTH Aachen University or at any other university of their choice. Another cornerstone of success and with a strong German dimension is the establishment of an innovative system of quality management. RWTH Aachen has succeeded in implementing an up-to-date quality system at GUtech to maintain teaching, training and the administration processes at highest German standards. These standards have been and still are spread over the entire work environment of the university and have become one of the assets of GUtech.

These impressive facts are all proof of the outstanding reputation of GUtech. During the past 10 years, GUtech has become a model for the whole region. The university's study programmes are characterised by the highest academic and research-based standards in combination with practical relevance and a focus on the needs of the labour market.

We understand GUtech also as a bridge between Germany and Oman as well as between Germany and the Gulf States. It is indeed the one and only exceptional German binational project in the Gulf Region. We have always considered the German-Omani friendship reliable and substantial, and we are looking forward to strengthening even more the academic exchange and cooperation between our two countries in the coming years and within this project. GUtech as an excellent and transnational university can be a major pillar and an added value for the transformation of the country into a modern knowledge society and in enhancing a partnership-based collaboration between noteworthy institutions of higher education in Germany and Oman.

Congratulations on your 10th Anniversary and your success story and all the best for a prosperous future of GUtech!

VISION AND INNOVATION AT GUTECH – THE EARLY YEARS OF A NEW UNIVERSITY

Prof. Dr. Barbara Stäuble, Deputy Rector of GUtech for Academic Affairs 2007–2012

The first time I was made aware of plans to set up a German University in Oman was in January 2006, shortly after a visit of Prof. Dr. Janos Urai, Professor of Structural Geology and Tectonics at RWTH Aachen University (RWTH), to Muscat. Because of my background in International Higher Education, I was keen on learning more about the project and decided to contact him. Thanks to his introduction, I met Prof. Dr. Michael Jansen, Professor at RWTH Aachen University and coordinator for the project of a German University in Oman, on 10th June 2006. This was followed by a meeting at the Grand Hyatt Hotel on 11th June 2006, in the presence of both Prof. Jansen and His Excellency Sheikh Abdullah bin Salim Al Salmi, who would later become the Managing Director of Oman Educational Services LLC (OES). It was during these initial meetings that I realised that the project of the German University in Oman was going to be a special example of its kind: it was bold, visionary and aiming at excellence in education and research. Over the coming months and years, I would have the privilege of contributing to the growth of this new University, first as Project Advisor and Academic Director reporting to His Excellency Sheikh Abdullah bin Salim Al Salmi(from June 2006 to November 2008), then as Deputy Rector for Academic Affairs reporting to the Board of Governors of GUtech (from November 2008 to July 2012).

For an outsider, it might appear that the period from June to December 2006 had resulted in little output. In reality, this 'Inception Phase' was an important and productive period, during which workshops were held—the first in August 2006 in Aachen and then a second one in October 2006 in Muscat—allowing members of OES and RWTH to continue a process that had started in

2005 and focused on brainstorming specific scenarios for the future of the University as well as reflecting on common values. As weeks passed and ideas were exchanged back and forth, a Vision and a Mission started to emerge for the University, which were aligned with both the Vision that His Majesty Sultan Qaboos bin Said Al Said has for the Sultanate of Oman and the 'Leitbild' of RWTH Aachen. Then followed strategic directions, governance structures and management responsibilities. Finally, timelines and financial plans were mapped out. All the outcomes of this consultative process culminated in a *Collaborative Agreement* between both parties, which was signed on 27th December 2006, under the auspices of Her Excellency Dr. Rawya bint Saud Al Busaidi, Minister of Higher Education, and in the presence of His Excellency Sheikh Abdullah bin Mohammed Al Salmi, Minister of Awqaf and Religious Affairs and Prof. Hans Küng, Emeritus Professor of the University of Tübingen.

From January to September 2007 followed a 'Preparation Phase', which focused on all the academic and operational aspects of getting ready for the first student intake in the academic year 2007/2008. In February 2007, a first Board of Governors meeting was held, during which Prof. Dr. Michael Jansen was appointed Acting Rector and Prof. Dr. Christoph Hilgers was made Vice-Rector of the young University, both based in Aachen, while I became the institution's Academic Director, based in Muscat. In March 2007, Ministerial Decision 9/2007 granted the right to form the Oman-German University of Technology, as it was called then, and stipulated a maximum period of 6 months to submit the documentation required to obtain the licence to operate the University. In the period that followed, I had the pleasure of working closely with Prof. Dr. Janos Urai, Prof. Dr. Matthias Jarke, Prof. Rolf Westerheide and Prof. Dr. Martina Fromhold-Eisebith to adapt the curricula of the four bachelor programmes taught at RWTH Aachen University to the needs of the

Sultanate of Oman. This required redesigning the curricula in a way that allowed students graduating from Omani schools to be able to achieve the intended learning outcomes, adapting the content of the programmes to make them relevant to the socio-economic context of the Sultanate, and translating all courses from German into English. It also meant developing the curriculum for an Intensive English and a Foundation Year programme. The required documentations (both curricula and relevant market surveys) were developed at breath-taking speed and submitted to the Ministry of Higher Education, who issued the licence to operate the University in August 2007. The first four programmes to be approved were: Applied Geosciences, Applied Information Technology, Urban Planning and Architectural Design, Regional Management and Tourism—all addressing fields of knowledge and expertise highly relevant to the economy of the Sultanate of Oman. Simultaneously, the four professors who developed these curricula became Inaugural Deans of the respective faculties within the University.

Parallel to developing the curricula of our first Bachelor and Foundation Year programmes, a team of dedicated staff—both academic and administrative—had to be recruited to ensure the successful start of the academic year 2007/2008. With clear ideas about our goals, but no students, no classrooms and no offices to show, this was easier said than done. Prof. Dr. Christoph Hilgers and I held our first recruitment interviews in February 2007, in the business centre of a hotel in Ruwi. It was an interesting experience to see how some applicants could immediately appreciate our vision, while others were overwhelmed by the lack of structures and the novelty of building a new university from scratch. As a rule of thumb, the longer our interviewees had lived in the Sultanate of Oman, the more they were confident that big and bold projects were possible. This unintended litmus test allowed us to recruit a small but admirable team of visionary and motivated employees, many of whom (Jiji Tom, Dr. Manuela Gutberlet, RK Nair, Fatima El Madkouri, Mansoor Al Shabibi, Lorna Nairn) are still working at GUtech today.

While recruiting our initial team, Prof. Dr. Michael Jansen searched for temporary premises to accommodate the University in its first years of operations, until a permanent campus was constructed. Several different buildings were assessed, in Shatti al Qurum, Qurum, Al Khuwair. Finally, the decision was made to use two beautiful villas facing the Gulf of Oman in Al Athaiba. When cyclone Gonu hit the coast of the Sultanate of Oman in June 2007, several of our staff members were caught in the middle, but thankfully no one got hurt and the University's premises were spared. Work soon resumed and, as the start of the new academic year approached, the foundations were laid for the University's future administrative departments: Information Technology, Human Resources, Finances, Marketing, Public Relations, Registration and Student Affairs, Library and Information Systems, as well as Health and Safety. During this preparation phase there also began a fruitful and continuous exchange with the Directorate of Private Colleges and Universities of the Ministry of Higher Education of the Sultanate of Oman, who provided us with valuable advice and guidance in the setting up of our institution and who have been supportive of our institution ever since.

On 6th October 2007, the University welcomed 60 students to its very first Orientation Days. At this point in time, the villas in Al Athaiba did not have a room big enough to accommodate such a 'large' number of people. I therefore had the pleasure of welcoming our new students in an airy tent overlooking the blue waters of the Gulf of Oman. The contrast between what was visible to the observer and what was envisioned for the University's future could not have been bigger. Yet all those present, whether student or staff, shared a common goal: to transform this young institution into one of the best universities in the Sultanate of Oman. The Orientation Days of October 2007 marked the beginning of the next developmental phase of GUtech, defined as the 'Initial Period' in the Collaborative Agreement. This phase began in the academic year 2007/2008, with the initial teaching of the University's Intensive

English Programme and Foundation Year, and ended upon completion of the academic year 2011/2012, with the graduation of the first GUtech Bachelor students.

In the following months, the team of academic and administrative staff expanded steadily as the framework was developed to support the growth of the University. Prof. Dr. Christoph Hilgers relocated from Aachen to Muscat in April 2007. Dr. Nicola Huson became the first German lecturer and focal point of the German Academic Exchanges Services (DAAD). A Student Council was established within the University as early as November 2007 and re-elected on a yearly basis. This provided the University with an important channel for student feedback that is still active and thriving today. What followed were productive years of interaction between professors and students.

THE EARLY YEARS OF GUTECH – FROM VISION TO REALITY

Prof. Dr. Christoph Hilgers, GUtech Deputy Rector for Administration and Finance 2007–2009

I gradually became involved with the vision of Prof. Dr. Michael Jansen and the Al Salmi Family to establish a university in Oman in 2005. Being with Prof. Dr. Janos Urai and his team in Geosciences at RWTH, we had been working for some years in Oman doing applied research and collaborating with industry. From day one Janos Urai was extremely supportive of the vision. I was thus able to join RWTH International Office to explore the potential at student fairs in UAE and Oman, and took part in several meetings with Prof. Jansen and other stakeholders alongside my daily work as Deputy Head of Janos' department.

In summer 2006 a project was set up, the lead given to RWTH Prof. Dr. Robert Schmitt from the Laboratory for Machine Tools and Production Engineering (WZL). I was about to leave university and join the international oil industry, job offers in hand, when this unique opportunity appeared to make a vision happen — to build a university in Oman from scratch. A Liaison Office was established at WZL, which I joined as executive director in 2006. Market surveys, project plans, investments, organization structures, quality concepts and contracts were developed by a small team and negotiated with the Omani representatives His Excellency Sheikh Abdullah bin Salim Al Salmi and Prof. Dr. Barbara Stäuble. Our first milestone was achieved in December 2006, when the contract between the Omani sponsors and RWTH was signed in Muscat. The project plan to establish a University in Oman was put into action.

In 2007, the first staff were head-hunted and many interviews were held by Prof. Dr. Barbara Stäuble and myself in a hotel in Muscat. With nothing but a vision in hand, we were happy to find people to contribute to the as yet non-existing GUtech. The organization structure was established with the Acting Rector Prof. Jansen based at RWTH Aachen, Prof. Dr. Barbara Stäuble as Academic Director in Oman, and myself travelling to and fro. The Beach Campus was constructed and the German Academic Exchange Service DAAD and the Goethe Institute opened their offices on the campus. Although I had by now been elected as Vice-Rector reporting to the Board of Governors and the organizational structure in place, it was the entrepreneurial team spirit that put GUtech on the map. Our first milestone was achieved in autumn 2007, when operations started with the first intake of foundation year students.

In 2008, additional construction, marketing and head-hunting continued. I relocated to Oman during the first student intake and the Liaison Office staff at WZL was reduced by half. Industry and DAAD were approached to contribute grants for GUtech students. During operation, highest quality management tools were implemented and the international accreditation of GUtech's curricula set in motion. Many delegations visited the Beach Campus. Our next milestone was achieved as planned in autumn 2008 with the first batch of Bachelor students enrolled at GUtech. With the start of the winter term, former RWTH Rector Prof. Dr. Burkhard Rauhut relocated to Oman to become the Inaugural Rector.

In 2009, GUtech continued to grow and options for a new interim campus were evaluated. Quality was assured through international accreditation by ACQUIN in summer 2009 and the first research funds were granted to GUtech. The operation was now up and running. The project was therefore closed and moved on to the follow-up phase. I returned to Germany, where the Liaison Office at WZL was closed by the end of 2009, the point of contact being transferred to RWTH International Office.

I am grateful that I was able to meet the right people at the right time, with their many different professions, skills and cultures. These lines are too few to allow me to name all the persons who need to be acknowledged. However, it is with great pleasure that I look on GUtech today, its driving vision combining excellent education and applied research. All the best!

STRUCTURES OF GUTECH

Dr. Hussain Al Salmi, Deputy Rector of GUtech for Administration and Finance since 2009; CEO of Oman Educational Services LLC (OES) since 2016

On joining GUtech in July 2009 as the person responsible for administration and finances I soon realised that I faced many challenges that required much time and effort, especially in regard to the lofty dreams and vision for the University.

I realised that much had been accomplished by my predecessor Prof. Christoph Hilgers, and the new responsibility was very challenging, but I was happy to have at my side the very best support team, in the Rectorate of Prof. Dr. Burkhard Rauhut and Prof. Dr. Barbara Stäuble.

AIRPORT CAMPUS
One of my first important tasks was to find a solution to the problem of limited space resulting from the continuous rise in the number of students. This exercise proved to require some serious thinking on the location, accessibility and most importantly the number of classrooms and facilities that a provisional building should offer to an ambitious university. The Airport Campus was the temporary solution that helped address the space requirements needed to cater for the students enrolled in the Bachelor programmes in the years 2009–2011.

GUTECH HALBAN CAMPUS
An ambitious and ground-breaking project was put to me: designing and launching the construction of GUtech's permanent campus in Halban. The bar was set extremely high from the outset. The project necessitated a pooling of feedback and basic requirements for a fit-for-purpose campus. Various stakeholders were involved in feedback sessions to garner inputs. Environmental elements including building size, orientation, wind direction, and sun exposure were studied and incorporated into the design to ensure natural cooling. The first draft of the master plan was already being circulated in early 2010. During the 18 months of construction, we were closely involved in overseeing the smooth and effective realisation of the master plan. GUtech Halban Campus was ready and open, on time and within budget, to receive continuing and new students in the winter of 2012. GUtech Halban Campus is a melting pot combining the high standards of German engineering and the cultural heritage of Oman. The campus has grown in stature and has received multiple awards. In 2013, the GUtech Halban Campus was named the Best Commercial Building in Oman and the Middle East by Construction Week magazine. In 2014, the building won the award for the Best Social Building in Oman. In 2016, the GUtech Halban Campus won the award of the German Design Council in the category of Excellent Communications Design—Architecture.

MANAGING FINANCES
GUtech is privately owned and funded by Omani visionaries. It is part of Oman Educational Services LLC (OES), an Omani Limited Liability Company that owns other education-related branches and subsidiaries. Financial sustainability is the biggest issue facing any privately funded higher education institution in Oman, including GUtech.

The government's decision to ease the cost of higher education to parents and students has resulted in a decrease in the number of self-funded students paying the University's published fees. In tandem, the number of recipients of government scholarships has soared to 90 % of the total number of enrolled students over the past 5 years. Consequently, there has followed a reduction in administrative costs, which tend to grow faster than instructional costs in most higher education institutions. At GUtech, all administrative functional areas, from IT and HR to procurements, are centralized and standardized. Average control margins are another aspect of organizational performance that has successfully been addressed as a cost control measure.

RESTRUCTURING

To ease pressure on the budget, the restructuring of the Foundation Programme into GUbridge, the preparatory programme for new school leavers, was the most pressing concern. The restructuring provided a framework for GUbridge to act as a standalone independent branch of GUtech. It was approved by the Board of Directors in 2014. With this, GUbridge gained autonomy and flexibility in managing its procurement and human resources while keeping the education quality standards under the control of the Rectorate. This restructuring has also allowed for GUtech's leadership—the Rectorate—to focus on the core activities of the university: education, research, and consultancy.

THE MAHARA PROJECT—CENTRE FOR SMART, SUSTAINABLE, INNOVATIVE AND VOCATIONAL PRACTICES

The Mahara Project is an inter-disciplinary research centre designed to operate as a research site for smart, sustainable, innovative and vocational practices. The Centre is an eco-friendly building that has been constructed on the shores of Musanah.

The Centre is built to provide a platform for researchers and students to conduct research on, and experiment with, different sustainable solutions to a host of environmental concerns.

On closer inspection of the Centre's site, contextual and environmental surveys were undertaken to identify the ideal orientation for the building. As such, the positioning of the Centre's blocks and labs in relation to seasonal variations in the sun's path and prevailing winds were built into the design.

Mahara is organised into various blocks stacked to capture north-easterly breezes, alongside appropriately sized windows. As such, natural ventilation in the buildings provides significant cooling benefits at acceptable levels. This therefore allows for a significantly reduced need for air conditioning. Provisions for installing photovoltaic panels to capture the sunlight were also made. Besides this, Mahara is also designed to expand its green agenda to a range of smart solutions, including water collection and irrigation, individually controlled light switches, and renewable energy sources.

Among other things, the aim of the project is to use information and communication technologies to improve the quality of life and to initiate research into smart building technologies and robotics.

CENTRE FOR THE HISTORY OF SCIENCE

The Centre for Science History displays a significant architectural character reflected in its monolithic facade. It is envisioned as a mediating element between past Islamic sciences and GUtech's programmes.

The main purpose of the Centre for Science History is to encourage learning and education at all ages. The Centre aims to introduce younger generations to science in an engaging and interactive way. Visitors can experience the wonder of science in the Islamic world through inspiring exhibitions, films and events.

The Centre is designed to host temporary events and exhibitions, but also includes a permanent exhibition on the findings of Islamic scientists and their scientific activities between the 9th and 16th centuries. The Centre focuses on mathematics, astronomy, geography, navigation, optics, mechanics and statics. It was completed in the summer of 2016 and is set to open its doors to visitors at the beginning of January 2018.

STUDENT LIFE AND SUMMER ACADEMY

As a university with a diverse cultural environment, GUtech has endeavoured to provide an appropriately varied student lifestyle. It strives to deliver a social and intellectual environment outside the classroom where our students can enrich their quality of student life, and make a positive contribution to our dynamic campus community through their unique experiences at GUtech.

We have managed to create opportunities for GUtech students to make the most of student life, providing events and activities that support their progress, fitness and success both within and without the classroom. More than 30 events are hosted annually at GUtech. These range from academic to sports and entertainment topics.

Students are spoiled for choice when it comes to social clubs. GUtech has over 10 social clubs for students to join, on and off campus, covering a broad range of subjects and interests, ranging from the Student Media Centre, a club devoted to creating media content and covering events at GUtech, to the Theatre Club, the club which has won most regional awards in off-campus competitions.

In 2015, GUtech hosted its first Summer Academy for young school students (from 14–17 years old) as a form of community service, conceived as a project for the Oman university. The programme has been designed and implemented by GUtech professionals, thus ensuring the highest standards in education, innovation and quality.

The programme has been continued by GUtech every summer since then under the name of GU Summer Academy, covering activities that develop the students' talents and broaden their perceptive in a fun way. It is built to suit Omani customs, traditions and Islamic life teachings, to ensure the highest degree of knowledge and comfort.

JOINT PROJECTS OF GUTECH AND RWTH AACHEN UNIVERSITY

Prof. Dr. Robert Schmitt, Member of GUtech Board of Governors since 2007

RWTH Aachen University has supported GUtech since its foundation in 2006. The first joint project *Foundation of the German University of Technology in Oman (GUtech) in Muscat in the Sultanate of Oman — Development of a Quality Management System* was started in 2007 and funded by the German Academic Exchange Service (DAAD). The goal of the DAAD is the internationalization of Germany's resource knowledge, the increase of the appeal of Germany as a university and science location and the fulfillment of important goals in development policy as well as foreign culture and education policy through education export. Therefore, the participation of the German Academic Exchange Service (DAAD), as an internationally recognised organization working with the Federal Government, was and still is of great importance, especially due to its experience in the field of international education systems and its knowledge of quality assurance systems. For a project of this scope, this cooperation is particularly crucial for ensuring quality standards. The partners involved in the project were RWTH Aachen University (Rectorate), the university administration and in particular the Chair of Production Metrology and Quality Management of the Laboratory for Machine Tools and Production Engineering (WZL) of RWTH Aachen under the leadership of Prof. Dr. Robert Schmitt as well as the GUtech Liaison Office Aachen on the German side. On the Omani side, GUtech and its sponsors (Oman Educational Services LLC (OES)) were the main contributors. The project lasted more than five years (February 2007 to December 2010; extension from 2010 to 2012) and included four work packages:

1. Structure and implementation of a quality management system (QMS)
2. Evaluation of courses and study programmes
3. Quality assurance measures for students
4. Development of a network for the continuous adaptation of teaching based on the needs of industry and society

The project started with the implementation of an appropriate quality management system (QMS) which was structurally designed after an analysis of the GUtech-specific requirements had been performed. The objective of a QMS is to ensure the quality of an organization's processes and system. The structure of a functional and powerful QMS usually originates as follows: After an analysis of the individual requirements of the facility, the corresponding target QMS can be structurally designed and the design of the process map can begin. The implementation is carried out by identifying and analyzing all processes critical to success, optimizing them if necessary and documenting them in a QM manual.

In order to guarantee the highest possible quality standards from the beginning, the processes which needed to be established at GUtech were based on those of RWTH Aachen University, but adapted to the special conditions on site. The close orientation to RWTH Aachen University was not only realised to guarantee high quality standards, but also to support the goals of the DAAD regarding the internationalization of Germany's knowledge, increasing the appeal of Germany as a university and science location as well as supporting policy goals. Hence a QMS was implemented that includes all sub-areas of the university. The focus was on ensuring the quality of teaching. In addition, parallel quality management and project management support have significantly bolstered GUtech's development process. The almost simultaneous start of the establishment of GUtech and the DAAD project was an important step towards securing the quality of all growing structures and established processes from the start. To this end, a stable and sustainable process structure was initially created and project management was started at an early stage in order to support current project activities and ensure project success within the defined time frame. The process map was developed in cooperation with GUtech employees. A process map gives an overview of the different processes of the organization, which are usually split into key processes (i.e. student registration process) and supporting processes (i.e. how to apply for a business trip). The approved processes have been implemented; processes critical to success (i.e. timetable creation or the allocation of students to classes) have been optimized where necessary. In order to ensure that information is readily accessible to interested parties, all relevant structures, processes, forms, responsibilities, etc. were made available to GUtech employees and students in the form of a web-based QM manual, depending on their access rights. Furthermore, to guarantee the future performance of GUtech, the web-based QM manual has been continuously expanded and improved in consultation with the Rectorate of GUtech and its employees.

Other quality assurance measures were carried out as part of the implementation of the QMS as well. In coordination with those responsible at RWTH Aachen University and GUtech in Oman, evaluation processes were implemented which evaluate the quality of the courses at regular intervals and derive improvement measures if required. The results of the evaluation are prepared and discussed in the Rectorate and with all employees involved. Measures are derived in a team, while the Deans and the Deputy Rector for Academic Affairs follow up the measures. Those evaluation processes were essential to later accreditation of courses. Additional measures to ensure the quality of teaching at GUtech have been implemented in the area of student support. Due to the still small but increasing number of students, this was still done manually. Based on absence and performance lists, a performance history can be tracked over the semester and, in the event of possible deviations, measures can be derived in consultation with the Head of Faculty/ Department or the Dean, such as the sending of warning notices or the arrangement of a meeting with the supervisor. The employees of the Department of Registration and Student Affairs are responsible for documenting the academic achievements of all students throughout the semesters, especially during the examinations. Deviations that occur are thus reliably identified and measures are derived. The procedure regarding the quality assurance measures has been recorded in various documents at GUtech and entered in the web-based QM manual. As a result, the percentage of students successfully completing courses as well as the percentage of graduating students continuously increased. Furthermore, GUtech's visibility in Oman and the Arab region was amplified through a large number of activities carried out in cooperation with the Department of Public Relations & Marketing.

The positive results of the project were confirmed during the initial evaluation of the funding project *Founding a Private University in Oman* as part of the DAAD programme *Study Programmes of German Universities Abroad* as well. The experts assessed the structure and processes of GUtech and conducted interviews with the employees of the university. In their final report they emphasize the importance of the implemented QMS for GUtech and its successful development and underline the significance of the project for their pursued agenda. As a result, a follow-up application for the project until 2012 was also approved.

In order to ensure high-quality teaching and processes at GUtech in the future, a separate quality management department was set up at GUtech (2010–2017). The efficient work of the QM department at GUtech requires a flexible, adaptable organizational structure for the department. This includes the definition of the connection between the QM department and the GUtech structure (e.g. staff unit, autonomous organizational unit, matrix organization). The special circumstances of GUtech at that time (e.g. two locations, strong growth) had to be taken into account and included in the planning. The performance of the QM department always depends to a large extent on the responsibility of the department. Therefore, clear task descriptions had to be specified for the employees of this department. This included the definition of which resources were available and which authorizations the employees had; this meant that the competences and responsibilities within the department and in cooperation with the other organizational units of GUtech had to be defined, coordinated and recorded. After that, the workload in the department was estimated. This is necessary for sound personnel and resource planning.

In the current follow-up project Step2Future (2017 to 2021) within the DAAD programme *Transnational Education — Study Programmes of German Universities Abroad (TNB-Studienangebote)* one of the main focuses is the further development of quality assurance at GUtech. The overall focus of the follow-up project is rather on organizational-structural and quality assurance measures. Above all, continuous cooperation and regular coordination should shape the further course of the project. Three main objectives have been identified to strengthen the established bond between the universities:

1. Consolidation and increase of the visibility of project results and the partnership in general
2. Improvement of intra- and inter-university communication structures in particular
3. Strengthening of the relationship to Germany

In order to achieve these overarching project objectives, four former measures will be continued and four new measures for the qualitative expansion of the project have been derived. In addition to quality improvement measures, these activities also include supporting GUtech i.e. in the implementation of a self-assessment tool for pro-

spective and new students. Furthermore, the development and implementation of supervision concepts for Bachelor's and Master's students, the implementation of further training offers for teaching personnel as well as the further development of the already established internship programme and the cooperation and project management accompanying all measures are realised.

The third overarching project objective, strengthening the link to Germany, is supported by all eight measures. For example, the quality improvement measures promote cooperation and intensive exchange between the German and Omani project participants in the areas of quality assurance and quality management. The mentoring concepts provide Omani students with an insight into German study conditions. They also bring RWTH Aachen University's students into contact with GUtech students and graduates.

The objectives and their measures support the successful development of GUtech and further nourish the fruitful synergies, past and present, between both universities. They are directed towards the TNB-STEP programme objective of addressing a German university (i.e. RWTH Aachen University) with GUtech in profiling its entrepreneurially oriented and already implemented transnational educational offers.

GERMAN UNIVERSITY OF TECHNOLOGY IN OMAN

Arch. Muhammad bin Sultan Al Salmy and Arch. Ernst Höhler,
Hoehler + alSalmy (H+S)

MASTERPLAN AND REALISATION OF PHASE 1

The GUtech — German University of Technology in Oman Project is managed by OES — Oman Educational Services and is designed and supervised by Hoehler + alSalmy (H+S) LLC (Previously registered as Hoehler + Partner (H+P) LLC).

The investment in GUtech's unique and distinguished design created an evident visual impact on the architectural pattern of its immediate surroundings — an outstanding landmark and kernel for the cultural and economic development of the project's location in Halban.

Aside from the well-known reputation of GUtech's educational skills, the project has captured all facilities required for the easy living of the users and inevitably the success of the project: campus catering, entertainment, accommodation and sports for students and staff. Given the elaborated habitat, the same has permitted flexibility for interior Omani residents to relocate comfortably on campus, in a secure area managed and administrated by the university itself.

The major architectural highlight is a large shaded amphitheatre with playing fountains and a seating capacity of 1,000, with a further 1,000 spectators able to watch the events taking place at the centre from the specially designed spiral ramps around the amphitheatre. Generous openings to the outside grant both inspiring views and natural ventilation within this inviting social space. The smart design allows the campus to expand in future if need arises. At present the campus can accommodate up to 1,800 students and it can be further expanded up to a total capacity of 10,000 students.

Furthermore, the success of the project has not been limited to the design and engineering aspects alone; the university provides unique and distinguished education for locals and welcomes exchange students from around the world. The project also enhances other routes on a diplomatic level and is considered one of the main exchange programme projects between countries.

The project involved meticulous designing, engineering and construction meeting high German and British standards, while accommodating Omani and GCC products in the construction wherever possible. It is not a surprise that whoever has seen, participated or worked on this project has experienced a new era in construction development.

The campus has been built in a way so as to use wind and solar energy in the most optimal manner. Energy efficiency is achieved by enveloping the whole building with thermal insulation and an air tight construction method of the facades. Along with Acoustic Sound insulation, these features ensure high international standards. Recycled water from the sewage treatment plant will be used for horticulture; green elements have been incorporated across the courtyards and campus to ensure the sustainability.

The construction of the project, with more than 50.000 GFA, was commenced in mid-2011 with a strict time schedule and fixed budget. All buildings, the main building with 527 rooms, 8 elevators, offices, lecture halls, laboratories, research areas, sports hall, canteen, cafeteria, shops, recreational areas and parking spaces, sewage treatment plant, roads and other services infrastructure and three fully functional attached accommodation blocks, were completed in a striking 18 months' time — within budget and with high quality. Despite this short period of time, innovative architectural and engineering details and technologies have been successfully constructed and commissioned.

Professional, international and extreme safety initiatives have been observed efficiently — evidenced by the fact that the project as a whole has been executed with zero reported injuries.

This campus is the first of its type in Oman: A fully established university campus — more like a little village — with future expansions and phases are planned to cater for the development of the project. The ambitious design combines the Omani cultural heritage, local conditions and the most up-to-date technical building standards — an example of what the Omani architectural identity can be today and might be in the future. The success of the project as a whole including its approach, goals, design, construction and the standing project portfolio, has grabbed the attention of many all around the world. The GUtech has been recognised as a diplomatic window and is considered one of the destinations of many ambassadors and prime ministers working on Oman international affairs.

PROJECT PARTICIPANTS:

Project main consultant:
Hoehler + alSalmy (H+S) (Previously registered as Hoehler + Partner (H+P))

General contractor for main building and infrastructure:
Larsen & Toubro (Oman) LLC

Contractor for student accommodation:
Douglas OHI LLC

Architectural design and supervision:
Hoehler + alSalmy (H+S) (Previously registered as Hoehler + Partner (H+P))

Project manager:
Hoehler + alSalmy (H+S) (Previously registered as Hoehler + Partner (H+P))

MEP design:
Majan Engineering Consultants

MEP supervision:
Hoehler + alSalmy (H+S) (Previously registered as Hoehler + Partner (H+P))

Structural design and supervision:
Simon Engineers & Partners

Quantity surveying:
Majan Engineering Consultants

Structural consultant:
Binnewies

MEP consultants:
Ebert & Partner GmbH & Co. KG

Traffic planning:
Schmeck Ingenieurgesellschaft mbH

Fire consultants:
Tenable — Fire Engineering Consultancy

PROJECT DATA:
Plot Area: 500,000 sqm
Phase one infrastructure: 178,397.08 sqm
Main building: 35,697.00 sqm
Student accommodation building: 10,500 sqm

PROJECT DURATION:
Design: February 2009 – December 2010
Construction: February 2011 – November 2012

FIG. 71/16:
Halban. View of the main GUtech
Building from the South West.

FIG. 72/16:
GUtech Building from the East with
the students' residence in front.

FIG. 73/16:
GUtech Facade. View
from the North East.

FIG. 74/16:
GUtech inner Atrium
from the North West.

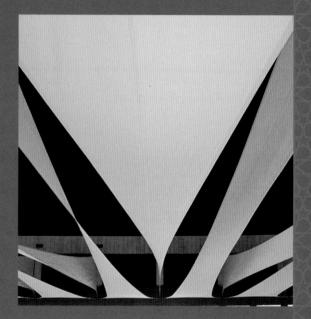

FIG. 75/16: Left:
GUtech students' residence inner corridor

FIG. 76/16: Below:
Sun sails' abstract pattern.

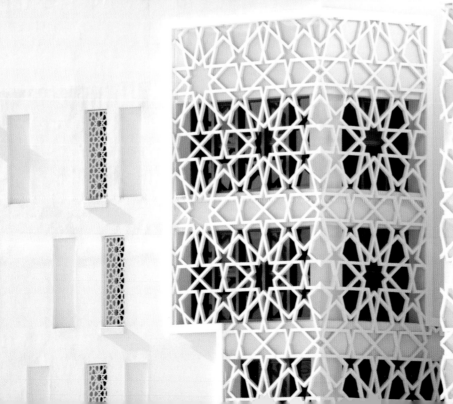

FIG. 77/16: Above:
GUtech students' residence inner courtyard

FIG. 78/16: Left:
GUtech students' residence curtain wall with Islamic pattern.

FIG. 79/16:
GUtech Atrium from the South.

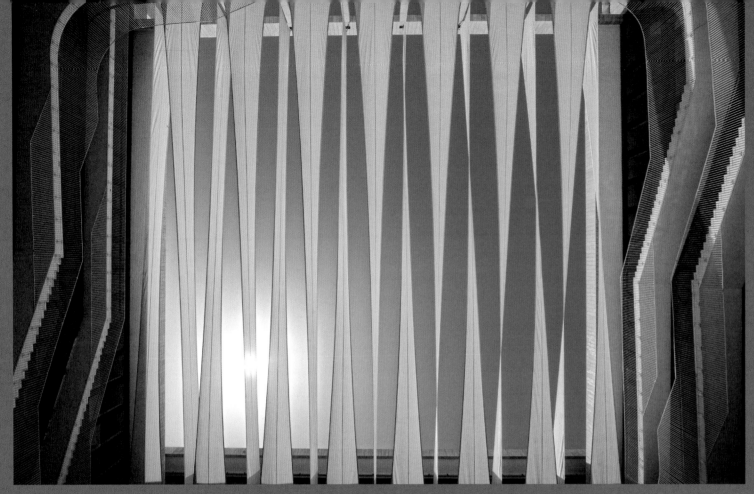

FIG. 80/16: Left:
Sun sails spanning
the Atrium.

FIG. 82/16: Opposite page:
Atrium from the South West.

FIG. 81/16:
Clockwise and anti
clockwise stairs and
ramps in the Atrium.

FACULTY OF ENGINEERING AND COMPUTER SCIENCE

Prof. Dr. Matthias Jarke, Inaugural Dean of the Faculty of Engineering 2007–2012 and Adjunct Professor of GUtech since 2012

Hundreds of dolphins greeted GUtech Rectorate and prominent guests on their boat ride outside Muttrah after the founding signature ceremony in the last days of December 2006. This feeling of great hospitality and desire to jointly promote high-level technical education in Oman accompanied the full five years from 2007–2012 where we had the honour and pleasure to serve as Inaugural Deans of the four initial Faculties at the German University of Technology in Oman (GUtech). Fittingly, the end of our appointment in December 2012 coincided with the graduation of the first batch of GUtech Bachelor students, in the just-finished new Halban Campus.

Digitization is now affecting all areas of work and life in Oman. Ubiquitous smartphones in everyone's hands, the Internet of Sensors in housing, traffic, oil and gas exploration and production are but a few examples. However, being more than a naïve user of digitization requires strong competencies, ranging from creative application development and business savviness to stringent mathematical and computer science foundations. Moreover, our graduates need to be able to interact with user organizations and specialists from many other disciplines, including all fields present at GUtech itself.

Based on such successful cooperation experiences, GUtech founders Prof. Dr. Michael Jansen and Prof. Dr. Burkhard Rauhut asked me to design a study programme of Applied Information Technology based on the Computer Science curriculum at RWTH Aachen University (currently ranked in the top 30 worldwide according to the THE survey). Prof. Michael Bastian helped, as Deputy Inaugural Dean, to add suitable business and creativity coursework. Already in April of 2008, we were able to hire GUtech's first professor, Dr. Nahla Barakat (databases and artificial intelligence), shortly afterwards followed by Dr. Lucia Cloth (technical informatics and communication systems) and Dr. Bernhard Heim (mathematics). Many internationally known professors from Aachen's Computer Science department supported the new group with course materials, fly-in lectures, and lab courses during student visits. In 2009, the programme was internationally accredited and first joint research projects started. In the following years, several senior professors joined GUtech, including Dr. Rudolf Fleischer, who—like Dr. Heim—had previously held research positions at one of Germany's famous Max Planck Institutes, and Dr. Basel Dayyani, after a distinguished career in the American IT industry.

Our small but excellent first group of students included an unusually high proportion of women. The first graduates demonstrated the quality of GUtech education by being accepted into attractive positions in industry or onto master programmes in internationally renowned schools. Nevertheless, to increase attractiveness, it was decided to rename the study programme to the more widely known Computer Science degree, without giving up the strong information engineering orientation which had already proven to be a major plus for our graduates in the job market.

In 2011, GUtech added several engineering degrees to its programme, and with the completion of my term at the end of 2012, Prof. Fleischer was appointed as my successor in the correspondingly renamed Faculty of Engineering and Computer Science.

FACULTY OF ECONOMICS AND PLANNING, DEPT. OF LOGISTICS, TOURISM AND SERVICE MANAGEMENT

Prof. Dr. Martina Fromhold-Eisebith, Inaugural Dean of the Faculty of Economics and Tourism Development 2007–2012 and Adjunct Professor of GUtech since 2012

When the Bachelor of Science programme Sustainable Tourism and Regional Development welcomed its first batch of students in autumn 2007, this set the start for educating young professionals enabled not only to design and implement new conceptual approaches fulfilling high quality tourism needs of Oman, but also to create solutions for wider issues of industrial development and investment promotion adapted to specific regional requirements within the country. The initial, already highly internationalized team of professors and lecturers included Prof. Dr. Heba Aziz (Egypt), Marike Bontenbal (Netherlands), Anne Soper (USA), Adrijana Car (Austria) as well as various 'fly-in' experts from Germany and other countries. This set of pioneer instructors represented a broad range of competences that all contributed to forming the students' and graduates' skills in analysing national and regional socio-economic wellbeing, visualizing relevant trends in the form of diagrams and maps, and elaborating viable concepts for tourism development and related fields. Besides times of intense learning and collaborative work in class, the various field trips integrated into the programme provided particular highlights for students and staff. They visited destinations both in Oman (such as Wadi Bani Khalid) and abroad (Germany and the Netherlands), which helped to deepen and add a practical dimension to the knowledge acquired in class through visiting tourism development organizations and companies in addition to designing and conducting empirical field work. When it became clear that a focus on tourism-related regional development was not sufficient for addressing real qualification demands in the country, the Faculty of Economics shifted its teaching focus and has now implemented new BSc study programmes on both Logistics and International Business & Service Management. Since then a growing number of graduates qualify to enter entrepreneurial jobs further promoting transport business and other corporate activities in the Sultanate of Oman and beyond.

GUTECH 10TH ANNIVERSARY – FACULTY OF SCIENCE

Prof. Dr. Janos Urai, Inaugural Dean of the Faculty of Sciences 2007–2012 and Adjunct Professor of GUtech since 2012

The opportunity to set up a Department of Applied Geoscience and the Faculty of Science in a new University in the Sultanate of Oman was exciting from day one (in 2003) of the discussions about this unique project. Oman is a geoscientist's paradise and integrating RWTH's ongoing research in Oman with an excellent local geoscience department was a once-in-a-lifetime opportunity. This way, we could train the next generation of Oman's geoscientists, combining RWTH's state-of-the-art technology with Oman's unique geological heritage, and thus contribute to the development of Oman's major georesources—hydrocarbons, water and minerals—and to the understanding of geohazards in the Sultanate.

I have many fond memories of the time which began with the Foundation Ceremony: designing the BSc curriculum; setting up our first facilities in the Beach Campus under the leadership of Prof. Dr. Burkhard Rauhut, Prof. Dr. Stäuble and Prof. Dr. Chris Hilgers; selecting the first library collection with Mansoor Al Shabibi; hiring faculty and building a team; integrating state-of-the-art geoscience into Omani culture; buying equipment; selecting an IT system with Jiji Tom; establishing a rock collection; and starting to teach our wonderful, courageous (and predominantly female) students. The hard work with our first team of talented and motivated colleagues Gösta Hoffmann, Anne Zacke, Ivan de Lugt and Michaela Bernecker, with strong support from RWTH Professors Peter Kukla and Klaus Reicherter, allowed us to create a university from the ground up.

I remember well the major efforts by Dr. Manuela Gutberlet in PR with public lectures, company presentations, school visits, together with radio and television programmes and newspaper publications, to build a reputation now well established in Omani geo-

science. Another milestone was the start of our first large research project with PDO, followed by several important TRC-funded projects, and the accreditation of our BSc programme. Perhaps the biggest surprise for me was the interest which came from the Aachen students, and I have fond memories of German students doing an *Auslandsemester* (study term abroad) in Oman, and of the geoscience field trips with both Omani and German students participating.

Now, after ten years, with a steady stream of students joining our courses, a growing number of alumni doing well in their careers, the start of an MSc programme shows the success of our concepts for education in the Faculty of Science. Our ongoing research, conducted cooperatively by RWTH and GUtech and published in a large number of papers in international peer-reviewed journals, has contributed to fundamental understanding and to practical applications for the development of the Sultanate.

It was a privilege to contribute to this project which has provided excellent degree qualifications for so many young Omani. I was proud to hand over the Inaugural Dean's responsibilities to my successor, Dr. Bernhard Heim.

FACULTY OF URBAN PLANNING AND ARCHITECTURAL DESIGN

Prof. Rolf Westerheide, Inaugural Dean of the Faculty of Urban Planning and Architectural Design 2007–2012 and Adjunct Professor of GUtech since 2012

In 2006, after some preliminary work by Prof. Dr. Michael Jansen and Karsten Ley, I was asked to develop an Urban Planning study course for the Sultanate of Oman. Careful and intensive research showed that there was no profound study programme of urban planning in the Gulf region so far. While architectural education itself was indeed present, the substantial foundations of urban design and urban planning skills had not yet been developed.

Society in Oman is confronted by many challenges concerning the entire urban and landscape spaces. Due to the demographic situation, the cities in Oman are expected to grow very rapidly over the next decades. The question is: What kind of city model will be successful and lead to a sustainable future? What kind of city will serve and support the lives of its inhabitants? The current trend of free-standing villas in widespread suburbs connected only through private transport is the most energy-intensive settlement pattern. Suburbs and highways eat up valuable land, traffic jams consume more and more time, and exhaust fumes poison the air. People living in suburbs are entirely dependent on cars, a phenomenon accompanied by a decay in health, and by social isolation.

In contrast, historic Omani settlements—take for example Al Hamhra or Ibra—were relatively dense structures with compact buildings and intact neighbourhoods, in which work, family life and recreation were integrated. The dense cities required less land, transport, and energy. But more importantly, they brought people together—a major source of innovation and creativity in society.

With university education we had the dream that future professional urban planners could help to realise another way out of the dilemma. In a compact city, where residential and commercial uses mingle, where cultural and educational activities are arranged in close proximity to each other—vertically or horizontally—people can live a physically, economically and socially healthier life.

The programme is tailored to improve skills and to strengthen the capacity for integrated urban planning and architectural design based on strong links to real-life challenges. Practice-related exercises and projects form the core elements of the curriculum, accompanied by state-of-the-art background knowledge and up-to-date planning methods, tools and techniques.

The recognition of Urban Planning as a profession close to architecture and landscape architecture is a basic requirement for a controlled and constitutive development of cities and regions in relation to their settlement structure, architectural and spatial forms, and infrastructure. Unique in the urbanistically very dynamic region of the Arabian Peninsula, the programme takes into account international and regional perspectives in preparing graduates for their task in dealing with progressive and sustainable urban planning in the international, especially the Arab-Islamic, context.

Along the lines of the study programme in Aachen, the core of each semester is an 'Integrated Project', a scheme which implements the various theoretical topics of the courses and lectures. This allows the provision of a wide range of techniques and professional approaches to the educational concerns and the integration of creativity, teamwork and communication as the most important qualifications for urban planning and architecture.

FIG. 83/10:
On the occasion of the celebration of the 40th Anniversary of
Oman's National Day GUtech students and staff form up to depict
the number 40 in Arabic numerals.

STUDENT COUNCIL

Gutech, as a brand new, aspiring higher education institute, soon realised that it was imperative to its success that the students' voice be heard. Once the Halban Campus was complete, the University's whole dynamic changed and it was of utmost importance to make sure that the students were not only settling in well but were also comfortable learning and gaining new experiences. The Student Council serves as the students' bastion of speech and first point of contact with the administration.

The members of the Student Council are elected by the students themselves and are only responsible for connecting the working bodies within GUtech—students and administration—with each other. The Student Council at GUtech has cooperated with the University's administration in issuing amendments to the Code of Conduct, has improved and revitalized the course representatives' initiative and liaised with the Student Affairs department regarding various events held at GUtech.

The Student Council's first task was assessing the fairness of the Code of Conduct and its applicability within the expected norms at the University. GUtech, being an international university, is a second home to students and members of staff from many different backgrounds. Taking local culture into account, this process must be dealt with delicately. The Student Council was given drafts of the Code of Conduct in order ensure its compatibility, as well as giving the administration an indicator of how the rest of the students could respond to any new rules introduced in the drafts.

As the year progressed, it became readily apparent that the course representative system needed to be improved. Student feedback varied between different courses and batches to the point where it was not feasible for a single student to convey the opinions and experiences of all groups undergoing different parts of their respective courses. Hence the Student Council elected one student per batch from all the fields of study offered at GUtech. For every field, all batches must meet and discuss what needs to be put forward to the upper management and a meeting can be held when necessary. So far, this approach has worked splendidly and letting the students voice their opinions in the most formal way allows the departments to swiftly operate with the given feedback.

GUtech is often said to be one of the universities most active outside academia with many events being open to the public as a result. These events include the National Day celebration, Charity Day and Earth Day. Naturally, students are eager to volunteer for such events and the Student Council members are the most engaged, even assisting where possible in the planning and organization stages of the University's events. The Student Council also helps attract more volunteers to help with the events by showcasing the fact that University events, when influenced by students, can even be more enjoyable.

CHAPTER 6
GREETINGS

Prof. Dr. Günter Flügge, Physics Course Coordinator
of the Foundation Programme 2007–2010

Let me first take the opportunity of this memorable tenth anniversary to congratulate GUtech on its great achievements.

More than ten years ago, when I first heard about the idea of establishing a private University in Oman, I was torn between enthusiasm and scepticism. I had always been fond of teaching, and doing so in an Arab-speaking country sounded like an extremely interesting opportunity. But I had never been to the Arabian Peninsula, so I did not really know what awaited me.

However, my first visit to Oman together with Chris Hilgers turned out to be a very positive surprise. A beautiful country with kind people, a small group of dedicated people gathered around Barbara Stäuble, and an enormous challenge ahead.

Ten years later I still look back with some nostalgia to my time in Oman, the enthusiasm of many of our students, the beautiful setting of the first location at the seaside, not to forget our weekend tours through the country.

Back in Aachen I had the opportunity to meet some of our first students several times and to learn, not without pride, of their progress.

HE Klaus Geyer, German Ambassador to Oman 2006–2009

On my arrival in Oman in summer 2006 I was quite surprised at the great number of interesting projects with German participation in the area of archaeology, natural sciences and education, all of them having a special character. One of them was the archaeological park of Al Baleed, an ancient port city near the city of Salalah in southern Oman. A pioneering role in its conception and realisation was played by Professor Dr. Michael Jansen from the RWTH Aachen. The Bochum Mining Museum was involved in the restoration of the important Bronze Age necropolis of Bat in northern Oman with its imposing 'beehive tombs'. Several German universities participated in an interdisciplinary project to study the oases of Oman. A huge botanic garden near Muscat, the first on the Arabian Peninsula and dedicated exclusively to the native flora and vegetation of Oman, was in the process of being established under the scientific direction of a highly committed German biologist.

In addition to its efforts to preserve its rich cultural heritage the Sultanate of Oman also attached great importance to the education of its young population, with a view to the future development of the country. German scientists and experts also worked in these sectors, both at the state-run Sultan Qaboos University and as consultants in the relevant ministries. A project undertaken in cooperation with GIZ focused on the development of needs-based training plans for various apprenticeships and the establishment of vocational training centres.

However, one project was really exceptional: the founding of a German-Omani private university, with the internationally renowned RWTH Aachen as its German partner. At first sight this project seemed quite bold, though I also remember some sceptical voices. But in this case, the long-standing cooperation in the preservation of the cultural heritage of the country as well as in the vocational and university education of its youth, combined with the strong personal commitment of the participating experts, had obviously born fruit and created a basis of trust, which made such an ambitious private enterprise possible for both sides. I am very pleased that during my tenure I could experience the first concrete steps of this initiative and that, from its provisional beginnings, a large modern university campus has become reality within ten years.

I would like to take this opportunity to congratulate GUtech on its tenth anniversary. All my best wishes for a bright future.

His Excellency Dr. Hilal Al Hinai, Secretary General of
The Research Council of Oman (TRC)

Congratulations to GUtech on its 10th anniversary and our best wishes for prosperity and growth in the years to come. I have been privileged to witness the development of GUtech since its early inception and interact with a number of its leading personalities. Within such a short period it has become a shining example of a quality higher education institute within the region, demonstrating the German striving for excellence within an Omani framework of peacefulness and tranquility. The educational model applied at GUtech has demonstrated success in integrating the theory to be grasped by the students with the application of that knowledge practically in its field of application. On the research front, GUtech has added a significant contribution to the research ecology in Oman in terms of quality and quantity despite its limited size. A good example of this is the EcoHouse built on campus, which integrated the knowledge gained from the vernacular architecture in Oman with latest technology in construction and solar energy. I am sure within the next decade we will witness a significant growth and integration of GUtech to be a beacon of knowledge and innovation.

Myriam Hoffmann, Instructor of the Creative Design Foundation Courses of GUtech 2007–2010 and Prof. Heiner Hoffmann, Professor of Creative Design Foundation Courses of GUtech 2007–2010

Students at Nakhal Fort

GUtec

A new University at Muscat which also serves as an academic and human bridge between Oman and Germany... and offers a home to tolerance, deep understanding and learning from each other.

What a forward-looking and courageous project!

We, my wife Myriam and me, were
given the task of addressing a key
element in German Higher Education:
creative thinking.

In fact it is part of our daily experience
as we constantly face questions and
problems without precedent which
we have to solve in a creative and
perhaps unconventional way.

„Creative Design" was our subject and
in order to always "practice what you
preach" we created new specific
programs which would spark
lively and original ideas.

We were not only pleased with
the results but also most grateful
for having met gifted and committed
students who are lovely and
open minded people.
All the best for the future!

Myriam
Hoffmann & Heiner
Hoffmann

Domkapitel Aachen
Der Dompropst

23.12.2017

Sehr geehrter, lieber Shaikh Abdullah al Salmi,

ganz herzlich bedanke ich mich für die vorzügliche Gastfreundschaft und die großzügige Aufnahme während der Tage unseres Besuchs im Oman. Auch Ihrer lieben Frau gilt mein Dank für Ihre Freundlichkeit und die gute Bewirtung in Ihrem Hause. Es sind für mich unvergeßliche Tage, die wir auf Ihre Einladung hin in Muscat verbringen durften. Ich bin so begeistert, daß ich im Jahr 2018, vom 16. November bis zum 25. November mit einer Gruppe in den Oman kommen werde. Ich danke Ihnen auch sehr für den kostbaren Weihrauch. Es wird unserem Aachener Dom ganz besonders gut tun bei den Feierlichkeiten des 40-jährigen Unesco-Welt-Kulturerbes im kommenden Jahr.

Wenn Sie zum Karlspreis 2018 nach Aachen kommen, lade ich Sie gern zu mir ein. Es ist für mich eine besondere Ehre, Sie als Gast in meinem Haus begrüßen zu dürfen.

Domkapitel Aachen
Geschäftszimmer
52062 Aachen, Klosterplatz 2
Tel. 0241/47709-112
Fax. 0241/47709-144
www.aachendom.de
Dompropst@dom.bistum-aachen.de

Bitte, geben Sie meinen Dank auch an all diejenigen weiter, die sich während unseres Aufenthalts in Muscat um uns bemüht haben.

Ihnen und Ihrer ganzen Familie sowie den Menschen im Oman wünsche ich den Segen Gottes für 2018 und grüße Sie herzlich

Ihr

Manfred von Holtum

Manfred von Holtum, Provost of Aachen Cathedral since 2014

Bruno Kaiser, President of the German-Omani Association, Berlin

10 Years of GUtech — a success story in the making

Ten years is a fairly manageable time frame. Nevertheless, the reasons for the celebration of this anniversary and for congratulations on the outstanding successes since the founding of the German University of Technology in Oman are obvious.

GUtech has confirmed and increased the good reputation that Germany enjoys in Oman. A look at the history of its founding shows that the university has succeeded in filling a gap in the education system of Oman. With its emphasis on technology, natural sciences and architecture, GUtech has helped to underpin and promote the goals of Omanisation, as promulgated by His Majesty Sultan Qaboos bin Said and his government, within the labour market of the Sultanate.

I recall with great pleasure a tour of the university campus, which showed how the university and its teachers and students have succeeded in combining traditional craftsmanship with the latest scientific and technological knowledge in the field of architecture. This is one of the success stories of GUtech: the reconciliation of the rich history and specific knowledge of Oman — accrued over centuries — with modernity, and the further scientific development of all these elements.

Since its beginnings, GUtech has enjoyed outstanding relations with the German-Omani Association, and has been actively supported by our member Prof. Dr. Michael Jansen. Prof. Jansen is one of the initiators of the university's founding; he was its first acting Rector, and he is still an important link between Germany and Oman. The good relations continue. Most recently, the German-Omani Association succeeded in placing Omani students in internships at both the prestigious architectural firm of David Chipperfield Architects Berlin, and at the Sto AG. The connections between Germany and Oman have thereby been strengthened at a professional level.

On behalf of the German-Omani Association, I would like to congratulate you on the 10th anniversary of GUtech. We look forward to continuing working hand in hand, consolidating links between our countries.

The German-Omani Association wishes the German University of Technology in Oman a successful future.

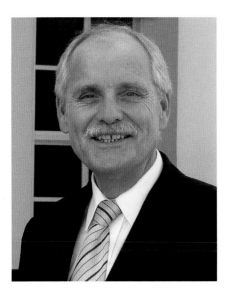

Cultures or religions, political ideas or social ambitions very often destroy the ideals of peaceful cohabitation. In contrast GUtech builds bridges between countries and people, between Muslims and Christians, between rich and poor. Although very young as a university, GUtech is in this sense a real success story.

I congratulate Sheikh Abdullah, all the Omani responsible for GUtech, the former and present Rectors Prof. Jansen, Prof. Rauhut, Prof. Modigell and all those at RWTH Aachen University who were responsible for making the GUtech story happen.

Moreover, I congratulate the students of GUtech who profit from the education at this German-Arab institution.

May the achievements of GUtech be an inspiration for politicians and entrepreneurs, scientists and students in the years following the 10th anniversary.

Dr. iur. Jürgen Linden, Former Lord Mayor of Aachen 1989–2009

The fact that the German-Omani project GUtech can celebrate its tenth anniversary bears witness to a unique and incredible success story. During this decade the initiator His Excellency Sheikh Abdullah bin Mohammed Al Salmi and his advisory team, together with a team from RWTH Aachen University, realised an idea resulting in a fruitful German-Arab relationship: the academic education of young Arab and international students by European and international scientists.

The concurrence of generations, cultures and directions of thought in this project provides not only the chance of common scientific progress but above all the substantiation of trust, of respect, of tolerance and all of the other European-Arab values reflecting a common basis.

Dr. Heinrich Mussinghoff, Bishop Emeritus
of Aachen Diocese 1994–2015

We thank you so much for this invitation to visit you personally and your country. I would be very glad to see you again in our town of Aachen and to welcome you to my house. I thank you for your kindness, openness and tolerance in wishing to create a good new world in which there is peace and friendship between our religions, and our countries can grow together in understanding, tolerance and partnership.

I pray that God may lead us to live in peace and friendship together. In the first Surah we learn to pray:

> *'In the name of God, the Lord of Mercy, the Giver of Mercy . . .*
> *Guide us to the straight path . . .'*

Sincerest greetings to your Excellency and to your families, to His Majesty and highly esteemed Sultan, to your country and people.

Manfred Nettekoven, Chancellor and Head of Administration and Finance of RWTH Aachen University since 2006

There is nothing more universal than knowledge. And there is nothing more precious than education. In addition, one could argue that universities are international by definition. Yes, indeed they are, and yet it is a rare phenomenon when universities build institutional bridges between people, cultures, different religions and societies. Hence it is with great joy and satisfaction that I would like to congratulate the German University of Technology in Oman on its 10th anniversary. What an achievement! What a great symbol of philanthropy, of universal understanding of what it means to guarantee a future for the younger generation in Oman, and what a great opportunity for my university, RWTH, to have found such a wonderful platform for the bidirectional transfer of knowledge, and for precious encounters between scholars and students from all over the planet.

In the realm of higher education, international activities started with student mobility. International exchange programmes had a major boost in the late 80s of the last century, when the European Union started its mobility programmes. Today, internationalization reaches further; it entails international faculty, an international classroom and many opportunities to cooperate with partner institutions from abroad. GUtech is designed for this more advanced understanding of an international university. It contributes both to the development of Oman and to a better understanding of many scholarly subjects as GUtech's programmes intrinsically encompass international components.

I am convinced that this institution will prosper, I am proud that my university is adopting a major role in the process and I wish all contributors, participants, students, staff and scholars the best of luck! Celebrate and be joyful and aware of this achievement, which is still a rare find in the global world of academia.

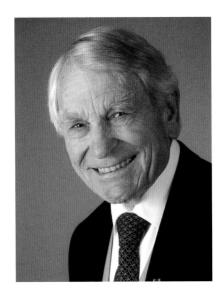

Dr. h.c. W. Georg Olms and Dietrich Olms,
Publisher Olms Verlag, Hildesheim

Georg Olms AG
Verlag
Hagentorwall 7
31134 Hildesheim
GERMANY

Telefon 0 51 21/ 15010
Telefax 0 51 21/150150
E-mail: info@olms.de
Internet: www.olms.de

10 Years GUtech –

My sincere congratulations!

It is impressive to witness the development of the GUtech during the course of years, and we do so with most respect.

We are very proud of the fact that a renowned German University of Technology of so much importance has set an example in Muscat in the Sultanate of Oman. Let me express my respectful and sincere gratitude to H.H. Sheikh Abdullah Bin Mohammed el Salmi, Minister of Endowments and Religious Affairs, who made an outstanding contribution to this year with its functional as well as fascinating architecture.

We also owe thanks to Professor Michael Jansen, Professor Michael Modigell and Professor Holger Rachel who joined this project.

With best wishes for a further prospering growth in the future.

J. Georg Olms

Hildesheim, 18th January 2018

His Excellency Hans-Christian Freiherr von Reibnitz,
German Ambassador to the Sultanate of Oman 2012–2017

Congratulations, GUtech!

10 years of extraordinary achievement and academic excellence have shaped Omani education in a very special way. Visionary and determined Omanis invited German university curricula expertise and organizational know-how to the Sultanate to establish a jewel of an educational institution — well known by now in the wider Middle East and beyond.

As former German Ambassador to the Sultanate of Oman I took pride in serving five years on the Board of Governors of GUtech. Seeing the University develop further since it moved to the Halban Campus in 2012 was all the more important to me as a proud father of a GUtech student. The combination of Omani educational vision and German effectuation is a unique selling point which sets quality above quantity. Today, with almost 2000 students, GUtech has outgrown its initial years and finds itself in the middle of a decisive phase of adolescence. While the first generations of graduates and alumni of GUtech already drive the transformation of the Omani economy, GUtech is focusing on sustaining and fulfilling the level of ambition and serving the interest of the Omani Nation. GUtech's competitive advantages are: demanding curricula, dedicated teachers, an environment conducive to learning, and students who understand that only competition will help them stand their ground in their academic and professional lives. Strengthening these advantages remains a continued responsibility.

10 years of GUtech give me more than one reason to wholeheartedly thank His Majesty Sultan Qaboos bin Said Al Said and all distinguished personalities engaged in the GUtech project, students, professors, academic and administrative staff, as well as all friends of the University for their active support. Together they all have created and shaped a unique and challenging space of learning, ambition, solidarity and friendship in Oman and an outstanding asset in German-Omani relations.

May GUtech continue to live, grow and flourish!

His Excellency Thomas Friedrich Schneider, German Ambassador to the Sultanate of Oman 2017–present

"Because the clear river of knowledge is one from which all should drink, and the channels flowing from it should carry richness, fecundity and growth to every part of Oman's pure and noble land."

With these words the late His Majesty Sultan Qaboos bin Said Al Said powerfully expressed the progressive thinking and open mindedness which characterised the cultural and intellectual environment that allowed for the establishment of GUtech back in 2007. At the time a group of Omani and German enthusiasts around His Excellency Sheikh Abdullah bin Mohammed Al Salmi showed the courage and leadership to make a vision become reality. When I took office as German Ambassador in Muscat ten years later, GUtech was already a well-established institution and an integral part of Oman's higher education landscape.

Since then many things have happened. The Sultanate of Oman has entered a new era under His Majesty Sultan Haitham bin Tarik Al Said. The country, the region and the world face new challenges. It does not need a global pandemic to realise that international cooperation between universities, scientists and researchers is more important than ever. For a high-tech country like Germany the promotion of international academic exchange is an essential factor of any strategy for the future.

Looking back on GUtech's marvelous achievements is a good opportunity to consider its future place in providing first-class education to the leaders of tomorrow. I am convinced that GUtech is well-placed and well-equipped to play an important part as an active member of the global academic community. Moreover, GUtech has become a well-known platform reaching out well beyond academia, in particular to business and industry. In order to address the next generation of high-tech manufacturing leaders GUtech has launched the Siemens Mechatronic Systems Certification Programme (SMSCP). By hosting the Oman Hydrogen Centre GUtech sets the course for energy solutions of the future. These examples highlight the huge potential for future synergies between higher education and business.

Yet what makes GUtech a truly unique place is the atmosphere of tolerance and togetherness which unites students, teachers, administrative staff and owners as one big GUtech family, making it a prominent flagship of German-Omani friendship in the region and beyond.

The German Embassy in Muscat shall continue to support GUtech in every possible way, and I look forward to engaging with the vibrant community of students and staff at GUtech in the future.

Her Excellency Angelika Storz-Chakarji, German Ambassador to the Sultanate of Oman 2009–2012

The 10th anniversary of GUtech Oman is a very special date for all those who were, and still are, a part of this remarkable project. GUtech is an outstanding example of how a vision can come true.

I vividly remember the year 2009, which is the year when I arrived in the Sultanate of Oman. During preparation for my assignment GUtech had been commended to my care as a pillar of Omani-German cooperation and as a role model for the whole region.

At the time GUtech was still in its infancy. Aspirations were high, and occasionally I was greeted with amazement and disbelief that such an ambitious project could 'fly'. However, I had the privilege to witness an idea come true which will serve so many generations to come.

I saw GUtech move from the beach villa to the airport building. I saw the ground-breaking in Halban and the topping-out ceremony. I saw the German Federal President visit the construction site of GUtech on the occasion of his state visit to the Sultanate of Oman. And I finally had a chance to visit GUtech in full operation when I was back in the Sultanate for a short visit.

Time confirms that GUtech's founding fathers were right. 2000 students at present—what a success story!

I would like to pay tribute to the vision and courage of these founding fathers and to their determination. I would also like to extend my sincere congratulations to each and every one of those in one way or another attached to this great institution of excellence.

May GUtech continue to flourish. GUtech will always have a special place in my heart.

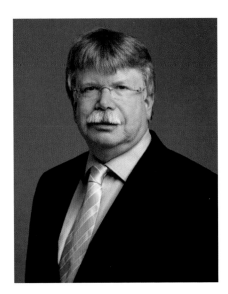

Dr. Michael Stückradt, Chancellor and Head of Administration and Finance of RWTH Aachen University 2000–2005

In my first few weeks as newly appointed Deputy Rector for Administration and Finances at RWTH Aachen University in March 2000 I already got to hear about the research activities of professors from RWTH Aachen University in Oman and their contacts to the Omani government and the government-financed Sultan Qaboos University (SQU). Their activities in archeological excavations and architecture led to contacts between the executive boards of SQU and my own university. Additionally, based on a common interest in the religious heritage of Oman, the former Deputy Rector of RWTH Aachen University, Prof. Dr. Michael Jansen, met the Omani Minister for Endowment and Religious Affairs, His Excellency Sheikh Abdullah bin Mohammed Al Salmi, and both intensified their contact.

On the basis of a Royal Decree concerning the possibility of establishing private universities in Oman the Minister Sheikh Abdullah planned to open a private university of technology in Oman, mainly financed by himself. His contact with Prof. Jansen entailed a visit to our university in Aachen where I met him for the first time.

I was impressed not only by his knowledge and his personality but also by his appreciation of foreign cultures and religions.

In the context of such encounters talks were starting about support from, and cooperation with, RWTH Aachen University regarding the envisaged new university in Oman. Obviously the Omani side appreciated the technological knowledge, the research spirit and the engineering know-how of RWTH.

At that time it was not unusual for internationally renowned universities to open branches abroad. Though other German universities had tried to follow this trend, no existing model seemed to meet both the specific situation of RWTH and the needs of Oman. A perfectly-fitting solution was sought in numerous talks within RWTH followed by consultations with the Omani partners. The question of funding was particularly significant; the engagement of RWTH in Oman should not be a financial burden on the German university. A first breakthrough was achieved during a visit in Muscat in the autumn of 2004 when the envisaged model was presented to the prospective Omani sponsors.

As a result a lively cooperation started, leading to the establishment of GUtech and the positive development of this university with German characteristics. Unfortunately I could not participate in this progress since I had left RWTH and had been appointed as Secretary of State at the Ministry of Science.

Cultural exchange is becoming increasingly significant, and the foreign involvement of German universities seems to me of great importance. As Deputy Rector of Administration and Finances of the University of Cologne—my present position—I therefore wish GUtech all the best, good luck and a long lasting and continuously successful existence.

CHAPTER 7
EXCURSIONS

FIG. 84/11:
DAAD study trip to Aachen in 2011 with (left) Mohamed
bin Sulaiman Al Salmi accompanying the group.

APPLYING THEORY IN PRACTICE, PROMOTING KNOWLEDGE AND BUILDING BRIDGES – GUTECH EXCURSIONS

Study-excursions are an important learning tool for GUtech students. Excursions are an integral part of all BSc and BEng study-programmes. What has been studied in theory in the lecture hall at GUtech should be applied and tested in the field or in laboratories. Right from the start of the university, professors from GUtech and RWTH Aachen have introduced local and international excursions and exchange programmes. The German Academic Exchange Service (DAAD) has supported numerous excursions as well as international workshops attended by a total of 562 GUtech students since 2008.

In March 2008, the first excursion to the Omani mountains was conducted with the first batch of ten BSc Applied Geosciences students and three visiting Geosciences students from RWTH Aachen University on a geological tour to Wadi Al Abyad (pictured).

One year later, in summer 2008, the first international GUtech excursion to Germany was conducted, a geological field-excursion with 10 students, which included a laboratory course at RWTH Aachen University and even a special visit to the German Bundestag in Berlin (pictured below).

Since that year Applied Geosciences excursions to Germany or to other European countries like Spain and France have been conducted on an annual basis. Since 2009, GUtech's students annually participate in the International Laboratory Course in Carbonate Microfacies, the so-called 'Flügel Course', held at the University of Erlangen (Germany).

The first joint Omani-German Architecture Workshop entitled 'Architecture—Tradition and Modernization' was held in November 2009. In 2012 GUtech and the London School of Architecture conducted a joint summer workshop that was followed by an exhibition outside the airport campus. In recent years students of the Department of Urban Planning and Architectural Design (UPAD) participated in the International Architecture Summer School in Berlin. The course has been organised in collaboration between GUtech, Iowa State University (USA) and the City College in New York (USA).

To facilitate a real world experience related to tourism, regional development and to interact with students from other partner-universities, the Department of International Business and Service Management (IBSM) has been conducting local, regional and international excursions, e.g. to Dubai, Bahrain, Croatia and Germany.

In Croatia GUtech students and professors have been participating in the annual International Academy for Tourism and Hospitality at Sea (ITHAS). Logistics study-excursions to Germany were conducted in recent years. While visiting various logistics companies (pictured below), the students learnt about supply chain management and how logistics work in different fields and on different scales.

In 2014 a group of Computer Sciences students attended an Android Workshop at the University of Saarbrucken. In 2017 a group of students learnt more about smart city projects and smart techniques at the University of Bremen (pictured).

There the group was introduced to various research laboratories such as the Bremen Ambient Assisted Living Lab (BAALL). Moreover, the students attended a workshop about the 'Internet of Things' at the renowned German Research Centre, the Fraunhofer Institute in Bonn. The students also visited the Computer Science department at RWTH Aachen University.

GUtech BEng students and their professor have been conducting annual study-excursion to RWTH Aachen University and to different industries in Oman since summer 2015. The main goal of the excursion is to apply different measurement techniques at the Engineering laboratories of RWTH Aachen University and to visit

FIG. 87/13:
MSc Petroleum Geosciences students and Prof. Wiekert Visser during a summer excursion to Dorset (UK) in 2013.

FIG. 85/08:
First Joint Applied Geosciences Excursion to Wadi Al Abyad with Prof. Dr. Janos Urai and Prof. Dr. Christoph Hilgers in 2008.

FIG. 86/09:
Applied Geosciences Summer Trip to Spain with Prof. Bas den Brock in 2009.

FIG. 88/13
Students from GUtech and from the University of Applied Sciences in Munich visited the Alps in 2013.

FIG. 89/11:
Geoscience Excursion to Germany 2011.

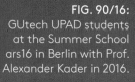

FIG. 90/16:
GUtech UPAD students at the Summer School ars16 in Berlin with Prof. Alexander Kader in 2016.

different chemical industries. The GUtech engineering students conduct most of the laboratory course at the Machine Tools Laboratory (WZL) and at the Department of Chemical Engineering (AVT). These laboratories are state-of–the-art engineering laboratories. The students get an idea about different university research projects and this experience may assist their future academic work.

Beside these programme related excursions GUtech students participate in culture and language excursions to RWTH Aachen University. In summer 2008 the first group of ten students travelled to Aachen for a two week course (pictured along with the former Lord Mayor of Aachen Dr. Jürgen Linden).

The students studied German in the mornings and participated in an intercultural student exchange programme with RWTH Aachen students in the afternoons, conducting various excursions to the surrounding areas of the city of Aachen. Due to its success the excursion has been conducted on a yearly basis.

Dr. Manuela Gutberlet, Public Relations Manager of GUtech

CHAPTER 8
SPECIAL EVENTS

FIG. 91/09:
Dr. Abdulrahman Al Salimi inaugurating
the exhibition 'Rembrandt in Oman' on
August 19, 2009.

SPECIAL EVENTS

The social and public life of the German University of Technology in Oman, GUtech, was from the very beginning full of social and cultural events which made and still make the academic life opalescent. University life should not be taking place in isolation. It is one of the primary responsibilities, also fixed in the Mission, Vision and Values of GUtech, to be open minded, tolerant and therefore, also interacting with the public.

Academic conferences, workshops, art exhibitions, annual social events, National Day Celebrations and public talks were and continue to be held at GUtech to engage students and academics with the community in Oman.

FIG. 92/09:
Illustration page from the Catalogue
on Rembrandt in Oman.

2009 THE REMBRANDT EXHIBITION

ABOUT THE EXHIBITION:
The event was an exhibition of 100 Rembrandt etchings from the Rembrandt House in Amsterdam (79 prints) and the Rumbler collection in Munich (21 prints), supplemented by three of the copper plates from which etchings were printed. The exhibition was held in the Afrah Ballroom of the Grand Hyatt Hotel in Muscat, which was subjected to a major remake for the occasion. (Gary Schwartz 2009)

REMBRANDT: THE MASTER AND HIS WORK
As early as in 2009 the Al Salmi Library together with GUtech arranged a sensational exhibition on 'Rembrandt in Oman'. The exhibition was inaugurated under the auspices of His Highness Sayyid Haitham bin Tarik Al Said on 19th August 2009 in the presence of many dignitaries and honourable guests.

'Rembrandt's paintings and engravings were renowned in his time, yet they gained even more importance after his death. These engravings are being shown in the Arab World for the first time, and they hold a special place among the creative works of the famed artist, setting a model that many artists have since then followed.' (Catalogue 2009: page 8)

FIG. 93/09:
Exhibition entrance area in front
of the Grand Hyatt, Muscat.

FIG. 94/09:
His Highness Sayyid Haitham bin Tarik Al Said cutting the ribbon jointly with His Excellency Sheikh Abdullah bin Mohammed Al Salmi.

FIG. 95/09:
His Highness Sayyid Haitham bin Tarik Al Said together with the honourable audience listening to the inauguration speech.

FIG. 96/09:
Chief guests in front of
the exhibition gate.

FIG. 97/09: From left:
The Dutch Ambassador to the Sultanate of Oman
His Excellency S.J.F.M. Van Wersch, His Highness Sayyid
Kamil bin Fahad Al Said, His Excellency Sheikh Abdullah
bin Mohammed Al Salmi, His Highness Sayyid Haitham
bin Tarik Al Said, the Director of the Museum
Het Rembrandthuis in Amsterdam Janrense Boonstra.

FIG. 98/11:
His Excellency the German President
Dr. Christian Wulff in discussion with
a student at GUtech.

2011 GERMAN PRESIDENT HIS EXCELLENCY DR. CHRISTIAN WULFF VISITING GUTECH

His Excellency Dr. Wulff, President of the Federal Republic of Germany together with a high-ranking delegation visited GUtech at the Airport Campus on December 10th, 2011. The President stressed the importance of education: '*Invest in education and in the competition of the mind [...]. We are deeply impressed with all your thoughts, [which you] even [express] in perfect German. I think you are [very well] prepared for future challenges,*' He further told the students, '*Unfortunately, your generation needs to solve problems committed by our generation,*' while adding: '*that it is important to look beyond each study programme and work in an interdisciplinary way*'.

FIG. 99/11:
The German President His Excellency Dr. Wulff amongst students of GUtech.

2012 TOPPING-OUT CEREMONY

Another highlight of the fast growing university was the topping-out ceremony at the new campus in Halban, celebrated in January 2012.

On this specific occasion, the Rectorate of GUtech along with its faculties and administration and the Board of Governors after its bi-annual meeting, the German Ambassador to the Sultanate of Oman Her Excellency Angelika Storz-Chakarji and the architects Ernst Höhler and Muhammad bin Sultan Al Salmy (Hoehler + alSalmy (H+S), then Hoehler + Partner (H+P)) assembled for the ceremony. Following the old tradition of the topping-out ceremony hundreds of labours and technical personnel working at the site, joined the celebration.

'*This is the biggest step in the history of our university. I am very proud to announce the new GUtech campus in Halban,*' said Prof. Dr. Burkhard Rauhut in his welcoming speech. '*Opening a university means approaching new horizons and shaping young destinies. It means changing the future by moulding the minds of young people,*' commented Her Excellency the Ambassador Angelika Storz-Chakarji.

FIG. 100/12:
The topping-out ceremony attended by: (first row from left): Architect Muhammad bin Sultan Al Salmy, Representative of the Contractor Larsen & Toubro LLC, Dr. Hussain Al Salmi, Mrs Inge Höhler, Architect Ernst Höhler, the German Ambassador to the Sultanate of Oman Her Excellency Angelika Storz-Chakarji, His Excellency Sheikh Abdullah bin Salim Al Salmi, Prof. Dr. Ernst Schmachtenberg, Dr. Dorothea Rüland, Dr. Christian Bode, Prof. Dr. Michael Jansen, Prof. Dr. Robert Schmitt, Prof. Dr. Matthias Jarke.

FIG. 101/12:
The Halban University Building
during the construction.

2013 THE PRESIDENT OF THE GERMAN FEDERAL PARLIAMENT PROF. DR. NORBERT LAMMERT VISITING GUTECH

The first top-ranking German politician who visited the new Halban Campus was Prof. Dr. Norbert Lammert, President of the German Federal Parliament (Bundestag). He was accompanied by Her Excellency Dr. Rawya bint Saud Al Busaidi, Minister of Higher Education of the Sultanate of Oman. 'The German President had a lively discussion with students from GUtech in one of our classrooms,' remembers Prof. Dr. Burkhard Rauhut, Rector of GUtech at that time.

FIG. 102/13: From left:
GUtech Rector Prof. Dr. Burkhard Rauhut,
The Minister of Higher Education Her Excellency
Dr. Rawya bint Saud Al Busaidi, the President of the
German Bundestag Prof. Dr. Norbert Lammert, the
German Ambassador to the Sultanate of Oman
His Excellency Hans-Christian Freiherr von Reibnitz,
on the occasion of the visit of the President of the
German Parliament in 2013.

FIG. 103/13:
Prof. Dr. Burkhard Rauhut presenting a painting to the President of the German Bundestag Prof. Dr. Norbert Lammert in the presence of Her Excellency Dr. Rawya bint Saud Al Busaidi.

2015 BESTOWAL OF THE ORDER OF MERIT OF THE GRAND CROSS OF GERMANY TO HIS EXCELLENCY SHEIKH ABDULLAH BIN MOHAMMED AL SALMI

One of the major highlights in the history of GUtech was the official bestowal of the Order of Merit of the Grand Cross of the Federal Republic of Germany on His Excellency Sheikh Abdullah bin Mohammed Al Salmi on 09.01.2015. The Order of Merit was awarded for his continuous involvement in creating cultural bridges between the East and the West. The ceremony of presenting the Order was undertaken in the name of the German President by the German Ambassador to the Sultanate of Oman His Excellency Hans-Christian Freiherr von Reibnitz in the presence of the Minister of Cultural Heritage His Highness Sayyid Haitham bin Tarik Al Said, the Minister of Higher Education Her Excellency Dr. Rawya bint Saud Al Busaidi, and the Minister of Foreign Affairs His Excellency Yusuf bin Alawi bin Abdullah. More than a hundred honourable guests from science, politics and economy participated in the ceremony.

FIG. 104/15:
The honourable audience participating in the bestowal of the Order of Merit of the Grand Cross of the Federal Republic of Germany on His Excellency Sheikh Abdullah bin Mohammed Al Salmi event. From left: Her Excellency Dr. Rawya bint Saud Al Busaidi, The Advisor for Culture to His Majesty His Excellency Abdul Aziz Al Rawas, His Excellency Sheikh Abdullah bin Mohammed Al Salmi, His Highness Sayyid Haitham bin Tarik Al Said, the German Ambassador to the Sultanate of Oman His Excellency Hans-Christian Freiherr von Reibnitz, His Excellency Yusuf bin Alawi bin Abdullah and further honourable guests.

FIG. 105/15:
In the name of the German President Joachim Gauck, His Excellency Sheikh Abdullah bin Mohammed Al Salmi, receives the Grand Order of Merit through the German Ambassador to the Sultanate of Oman His Excellency Hans-Christian Freiherr von Reibnitz. 'Germany is a great nation – diverse and advanced, with a rich history and culture. We feel huge admiration and affection for this enchanting and thriving country,' said His Excellency Sheikh Abdullah bin Mohammed Al Salmi in his speech of thanks.

FIG. 106/17:
Aerial view of the History
of Science Centre with the
'astronomic piazza' in front of
the main University building.

FIG. 107/17:
The double stairs in the
History of Science Centre.

2017 HISTORY OF SCIENCE CENTRE

Following the completion of the main Halban building in 2012, the History of Science Centre now lines the large square in front of the main university building to its south. Another teaching building containing laboratories lines the square to its north. The southern part of the square right in front of the History of Science Centre hosts several astronomic instruments, such a sundial. Lines on the pavement demarcate latitudes and longitudes. Within this astronomic setting beautiful water fountains and waterways along with date trees decorate the place in front of both the University building and the Science Centre.

The building itself consists of an interior unit enclosed by an outer decorative 'Curtain Wall' reflecting Islamic patterns. The simplicity in white of the Inner hall is impressive and is in contrast with the dark, wooden floor, slightly sloping from south to north. The slight sloping induces the visitor in an unfamiliar way to move from the higher southern part towards the lower north opening to the square. A double staircase leads counter ascending to the first floor where currently the scientific exhibition is hosted. Outside, in its north-western corner between the glass façade and the curtain wall, a wooden dhow is exhibited. A copy of an ancient depiction, it has been built with traditional techniques by 'stitching' the wooden planks by ropes without using any iron.

FIG. 108/17:
The Boat Model in front of the
History of Science Centre.

FIG. 109/17:
After the completion of the solitaire architecture of the History of Science Centre designed by Hoehler + alSalmy (H+S) (then Hoehler + Partner (H+P)), the Building had been inaugurated under the auspices of His Highness Sayyid Haitham bin Tarik Al Said (middle) in the presence of numerous honourable guests amongst which the Nobel Prize Winner in Physics (2014) Prof. Dr. Hiroshi Amano (second from right).

THE INAUGURATION OF THE HISTORY OF SCIENCE CENTRE AT GUTECH HALBAN CAMPUS ON DECEMBER 27TH, 2017

Chief speaker of the event was the Nobel Prize Winner in Physics (2014), Prof. Dr. Hiroshi Amano. He is a Doctor of Engineering, Director of the Centre for Integrated Research of Future Electronics (URFE) at the Institute of Materials and Systems for Sustainability (IMaSS) and Director of the Akasaki Research Centre at Nagoya University (Japan).

Prof. Dr. Hiroshi Amano was awarded the Nobel Prize in Physics jointly with his colleagues Prof. Dr. Isamu Akasaki and Prof. Dr. Shuji Nakamura in 2014. The three scientists received the Nobel Prize for their invention of efficient blue light-emitting diodes which has enabled bright and energy-saving white light sources, LED lights. Prof. Dr. Amano initiated a network of scientists who works on the 'Internet of Energy' a few years ago. The so-called 'Future Wireless Power Transmission Network' is an open innovation platform that develops sustainable, smart solutions for future energy challenges of our societies. According to Prof. Dr. Amano, by using LED light, Japan reduced its annual electricity consumption by 7%. Energy efficient LED lights contributed to the reduction of CO_2 emissions and global warming.

FIG. 110/17:
Chief speaker of the event, Nobel Prize Winner in Physics (2014), Prof. Dr. Hiroshi Amano.

FIG. 111/17:
His Highness Sayyid Haitham bin Tarik Al Said in discussion with the physicist Professor Pierre Coullet, Nice University and member of the scientific committee under the leadership of Mathematician and Historian of science Prof. Roshdi Rashed for the preparation of the History of Science Centre.

It was Prof. Roshdi Rashed, an eminent scholar of CNRS, Paris, who worked out the scientific concept for the collection. He writes:

'For more than five centuries, science was one of the components of Islamic civilization, both in schools, observatories, mosques and hospitals, and in connection with exchanges. Indeed, from the 9th to the 15th century, scientific research was fruitful and dynamic in most of Islamic cities.

To know and to make known this scientific heritage does not intend to bring back the dead nor to revive the past. The aim is to rekindle the nation's memory, so it carries on the scientific tradition, being driven by the values of knowledge which will enlighten the modern Islamic city, its universities and its institutions. The foundation of Centres for the study of history of sciences and Museums of sciences and techniques is one of the most effective means of diffusion of scientific culture.

The Muscat History of Science Centre and Museum's mission is to present the achievements of the scholars of this era in the field of exact sciences such as mathematics, astronomy, optics, mechanics, statics and mathematical geography, to make clearer, objectively and rigorously, the scientific foundations underlying these results. It is the first centre for the history of sciences in Islam that meets these scientific standards, in order to provide to a broad public the testimony of centuries of scientific research in Islamic civilization.

Brigitte Alix (Paris), Faiza Bancel (Paris), Giovanni Casini (Rome), Laura Catastini (Rome), Pierre Coullet (Nice), Jean-Charles Ducène (Paris), Jean Luc Filippi (Nice), Franco Ghione (Rome), Marc Goutaudier (Paris), Philippe Guillemet (Paris), Régis Morelon (Paris), Denis Savoie (Paris) and Eric Staples (Emirates), all of them academic scholars and researchers, each in his specialty, have conceived and created the Museum artifacts. Some of them have contributed to the drafting of some chapters of the Museum's catalogue.

I wish to thank especially His Excellency Sheikh Abdullah bin Mohammed Al Salmi, who asked me to think up the project of this Centre and its Museum in the neighborhood of the Technical University he founded, and to steer its realization; His Excellency has generously helped its construction. I would also like to thank Abdulrahman Al Salimi et Hussain Al Salmi, who have supervised all the steps of the realization of the Muscat Museum'.

FIG. 112/17:
Prof. Roshdi Rashed explaining the exhibition (from the film for the Exhibition of the History of Science Centre).

FIG. 113/17:
His Highness Sayyid Haitham bin Tarik
Al Said in front of a traditional sample
of ship planks stitched with ropes.

FIG. 114/17:
View of the permanent exhibition.

FIG. 115/17:
His Excellency Sheikh Abdullah bin Mohammed Al Salmi presenting a gift to His Highness Sayyid Haitham bin Tarik Al Said.

FIG. 116/09:
Inauguration of the Oman Exhibition in honour of His Excellency Sheikh Abdullah bin Mohammed Al Salmi at Sparkasse Aachen in May 2009.

FIG. 117/09:
Oman Exhibition at Sparkasse Aachen in May 2009.

OTHER ACTIVITIES

2008

Geosciences and Geohazards was the topic of a public career counselling seminar held on 4th May 2008. Professor Dr. Janos Urai, Inaugural Dean of the Faculty of Science, Head of the Department of Geosciences at GUtech and Professor at RWTH Aachen University, spoke about his fascination for the geosciences.

2009

On 9th May 2009 GUtech held **its first Open Day** on their Beach Campus premises in Al Athaiba. They were pleased to welcome around 1100 visitors over the course of the day. In total RO 1,800 was raised for local charities including Dar Al Atta and the Children's Public Library.

On 19th May 2009 RWTH Aachen University of Technology in cooperation with Sparkassse Aachen opened an exhibition in the rooms of Sparkasse Aachen in honour of His Excellency Sheikh Abdullah bin Mohammed Al Salmi and GUtech. With more than 50 photo boards the life of Muscat and Oman was presented for two weeks to the public.

2010

In October 2010 **The Muscat Green Conference — Education for a Sustainably Built Environment** was co-organised by GUtech. The event was part of a series of regional conferences on green building and environment conservation strategies.

2011

On December 11th 2011 the German Language Department of GUtech held its **annual German evening**, linked with a pre-farewell event for the first batch of GUtech graduates. The evening entitled 'Neue Horizonte — New Horizons' took place at the Airport Campus. The students had prepared German-language theatre plays, German pop-songs, poems and a video with interviews. 'I love to study German,' said Nusaiba Al Sulaimani, a first-year student on the BSc Applied IT course. Last summer, at the end of her Foundation Year Programme, Nusaiba was chosen to attend a three-week culture and language summer course at RWTH Aachen University.

2012

The first Engineering Conference was held at GUtech in January 2012. A large number of industry representatives, academics and students attended the one-day conference, which was organised in cooperation with RWTH Aachen University. 'Engineers shape our everyday lives. Engineers will be required to find solutions for global challenges such as renewable energies and water scarcity,' (Prof. Dr. Burkhard Rauhut) 'Engineering means designing the world of technology,' said Prof. Dr. Ernst Schmachtenberg, Rector of RWTH Aachen University, while Prof. Dr. Robert Schmitt, Inaugural Dean of Mechanical Engineering at GUtech and Head of the Laboratory for Machine Tools and Production Engineering (WZL) of RWTH Aachen stated 'Limited supplies of resources of primary energy and strategic raw materials will place a new dimension of stress upon modern production technology.'

2013

In cooperation with ETH Zürich, Studio Basel, the Department of Urban Planning and Architectural Design (UPAD) held a joint symposium entitled **Urban Oman—Urban Design, Geography and Planning in the Wider Muscat Region** in March 2013. Another workshop entitled **Building/Art/Invention** was held on exploring and experimenting with local materials, using traditional building knowledge to invent new materials for a future building material industry and new markets in the Sultanate of Oman.

The start of the **construction of the EcoHouse** was celebrated in October 2013 in the presence of the German Ambassador to the Sultanate of Oman, His Excellency Hans-Christian Freiherr von Reibnitz. The design of the EcoHouse is based on a student project that was realised by GUtech professors and UPAD graduates along with consultants, contractors, craftsmen and other companies. The EcoHouse is part of a student competition initiated by The Research Council (TRC). 'Saving energy is an issue around the world. Eco-houses have become a standard in Germany. Today we witness the construction of the first of its kind building in Oman. The project links German expertise and Omani building traditions,' said the Ambassador.'

In March 2013 the **Schlumberger Geosciences Laboratory** was inaugurated and collaboration was launched. Schlumberger Oman & Co LLC donated computer software Petrel and PetroMod, which helps to discover oil reservoirs and to optimise the petroleum recovery. 'PetroMod reconstructs geological history in time: when, where and how the oil was formed in the subsurface,' said Prof. Dr. Wiekert Visser, Head of the MSc Programme in Petroleum Geosciences.

FIG. 118/12:
First engineering conference held at the 'Airport' Campus in 2012. Prof. Dr. Michael Modigell in discussion with Prof. Dr. Burkhard Rauhut and the audience.

FIG. 119/10:
Geoscience Students in Germany in 2010.

2014

In cooperation with Sultan Qaboos University (SQU), a conference on the **Challenges of Urbanization in Arab Gulf Countries** was held at GUtech in March 2014. This conference was the result of an interdisciplinary research project on Sustainable Urbanisation Patterns in Oman, funded by the Research Council (TRC).

The 13th International Conference on Semi-Solid Processing of Alloys and Composites, the S2P Conference, with participants from around the world, was held in September 2014.

Documenting the fast-changing morphology of building structures of forts and castles in the Sultanate, an exceptional **fine arts exhibition** *Bridging Science and Arts* was held in February 2014. It showcased the artistic research project of Prof. Gazmend Kalemi of the Department of Urban Planning and Architectural Design.

2015

The 12th International Conference on Fossil Corals and Sponges took place in February 2015 at GUtech. Around 40 scientists from around the world participated in the conference

Several other public talks, such as the **Tuesday Tourism Talks** have been held on campus in recent years, organised by the Department of International Business and Service Management (IBSM). One of these talks, held by Prof. Dr. Nevenka Čavlek, was 'Experiencing Tourism Studies at Sea', on the International Academy of Tourism and Hospitality at Sea (ITHAS), a live tourism laboratory that combines travelling at sea and the study of tourism.

Under the slogan 'Celebrate Tourism: Oman is a Nation of Travellers', a special event was organised by the department in January 2015. Representatives from the public and private sector attended the evening event. 'Tourism and hospitality are close to our Arab culture and nature,' said Prof. Dr. Heba Aziz, Head of the Department.

To promote research on historic ship building techniques, the **first traditional Sewn Boat Workshop** entitled Fibre and Wood: Sewn Boat Construction Techniques through Time was held at GUtech in February 2015. The sewn boat technology was responsible for facilitating a wide range of maritime cross-cultural encounters in the past. The model boat exhibited at the Science Centre is a good example.

2017

GUtech was honoured by **the visit of Prof. Dr. Hiroshi Amano, the Nobel Prize Winner for Physics (2014)**, who gave a public lecture entitled 'Brighter World and Sustainable Life with Blue LED and Transformative Electronics'. Prof. Dr. Hiroshi Amano was awarded the Nobel Prize for Physics jointly with two other Japanese scientists. The three researchers received the prize for their invention of efficient blue light-emitting diodes which have enabled bright and energy-saving white light sources, the well-known LED lights. Prof. Dr. Hiroshi Amano is a Doctor of Engineering; he is the Director of the Centre for Integrated Research of Future Electronics (URFE) at the Institute of Materials and Systems for Sustainability (IMaSS) and of the Akasaki Research Centre at Nagoya University.

The 3rd International Symposium on Flash Floods in Wadi Systems was held with many international participants at GUtech in December 2017. At the end of the conference the organisers released a list of recommendations for the mitigation of flooding and disastrous damages in arid countries, including Oman. The first international joint SQU-GUtech Workshop in Mathematics took place with 40 experts in number theory from Japan, Germany, Oman, France, Saudi-Arabia, Turkey, Lebanon and India attending the workshop.

Another international workshop that attracted international participants and international media attention was the **AA Muscat Visiting School** organised at GUtech. Students from UK, Oman, Pakistan, Iran and Taiwan participated in the one-week workshop with the theme 'patterns'. Throughout the workshop the students were inspired to think out of the box, beyond their usual studies. Different kinds of techniques were used to create folded, hanging or woven structures. 'The idea is that students are like seeds that will grow and make the architects of the future,' said Omid Kamvari, Architect and Director of the AA Muscat Visiting School.

CELEBRATIONS AND ORIENTATION DAYS

National Day is celebrated is marked every year on November 18th. Traditional poems, songs and dances like al-Bara and al-Aazi are performed by students and staff members. 'For Omanis this day is the turning point of Oman. We are celebrating the achievements of our nation under the wise leadership of His Majesty and it is an opportunity for all of us to showcase our role as a university and at the same time to remind ourselves to participate in developing the country. This can be achieved through implementing our vision and sticking to our Omani values,' (Dr. Hussain Al Salmi, Vice-Rector for Administration and Finance, Speech on 18.11.2017).

Each year during its **Orientation Days** GUtech welcomes a new batch of students entering the Foundation Year, Bachelor of Science and Bachelor of Engineering programmes. On October 9th 2007 the young university, at that time named 'OGtech', concluded the orientation days with a **buffet dinner at its premises** in North Al Gubrah. About 130 people including OGTech students, their families and OGTech staff attended the dinner. The highlights were motivational speeches of four role models from the fields of geology, architecture, information technology, and regional management and tourism.

The **Charity Food Festivals** have been held annually to celebrate the diversity of cultures and cuisines on campus. **International Cultural Nights** were celebrated in 2014 and in 2018. The events were organised to showcase the rich cultural diversity. Stating Aysha Albright, students affairs executive: 'Considering conflicts and a sense of distrust and intolerance increasingly becoming the norm, no efforts should be spared to bring together various cultures to facilitate meaningful dialogue and mutual understanding and respect.' Each year several students and staff members have

been recognised for their **sports and work achievements**. For example, the GUtech football, futsal and female basketball teams all received awards. GUtech offers more than 15 sports, fitness and recreational activities on a regular weekly basis. To promote sports activities in the community, a public Basketball 3on3 Charity Competition was held jointly with the Oman Basketball Association (OBA) in February 2014.

FIG. 120/14:
National Day celebration 2014.

FIG. 121/09:
First Batch of GUtech
BSc Computer Science
(then Applied Information
Technology) students in the
snow during a visit to RWTH
Aachen University in 2009.

FIG. 122/13:
Graduation Ceremony 2013

CHAPTER 9
GRADUATION CEREMONIES

**"WE WERE PIONEERS.
WE RECEIVED AN EDUCATION IN LIFE."**

2012

GUTECH CELEBRATED ITS GRADUATION CEREMONIES THROUGHOUT THE PAST SIX YEARS

GUtech held its first graduation ceremony at the new campus in Halban on 8 December 2012. 30 Bachelor of Science students graduated in different programmes. GUtech staff, students, families of graduates as well as the German Ambassador to the Sultanate of Oman His Excellency Hans-Christian Freiherr von Reibnitz and other dignitaries attended the ceremony in the large open-air amphitheater of GUtech. 'Five years ago, we started with 60 students in the Foundation Year. Twelve graduates have already found a job, four are studying a Master's degree in Europe, two of them at RWTH Aachen University,' said Professor Dr. Burkhard Rauhut, Rector of GUtech. 'Our task is to enable you to adapt yourself to the ever changing needs of your future profession. Nowadays finding facts is easy but transferring them into knowledge to make use of it, is hard work. To be successful in your careers, you will need knowledge, imagination and passion for your work,' said Professor Rauhut.

In the graduates' response, Aysha Farooq, Amjaad Al Hinai and Hamda Al Hajri said: 'At GUtech we learnt punctuality from the Germans and the Germans learnt to say *in shah' Allah*. We were pioneers of the university. We spent long hours working and achieving our goals and we fell in love with our majors. We learnt how to question instead of receiving only answers. And in addition to our education we received an education in life. We proved that we are willing to learn.'

2012
APPLIED GEOSCIENCES

Kawther Al Quraishi   Sara Al Balushi   Hiyam Al Kindi   Noora Al Balushi   Aisha Al Riyami

2012
APPLIED INFORMATION TECHNOLOGY

Azmat Arif

Nourhan Al Okbi

Sarah Hawi

2012
SUSTAINABLE TOURISM AND REGIONAL DEVELOPMENT

Khalid Al Wardi

Amal Al Harthy

Lovelyn Aranha

Amjaad Al Hinai

Tariq Maqbool

2012
URBAN PLANNING AND ARCHITECTURAL DESIGN

Dalal Mohammed

Zainab Al Barwani

Rumana Al Othman

Ahmed Al Amr

Talal Al Umairi

Zainab Al Ghabshi

Hamda Al Hajri

Bushra Al Mani

Ghadeer Al Ghazali

Kinan Marei

Maha Al Salti

Sandy Bassett

Ali Al Mughairi

Rowa El Aamin

Aysha Farooq

Nushrat Alam

Rania Baig

FIG. 123/12: Above left: Graduation 2012. (From left) RWTH Rector Prof. Dr. Ernst Schmachtenberg, GUtech Rector Prof. Dr. Burkhard Rauhut, 2012 UPAD Graduate Zainab Al Ghabshi receiving her Bachelor certificate.

FIG. 124/12: Above right: Graduation 2012. Arena.

FIG. 125/12: Graduation 2012. (From left) Prof. Dr. Barbara Stäuble, Prof. Dr. Burkhard Rauhut, Prof. Dr. Matthias Jarke, Prof. Dr. Janos Urai, Prof. Rolf Westerheide.

FIG. 126/12:
Graduation 2012 with members of the
Rectorate and the Board of Governors.

2013

SECOND GRADUATION CEREMONY

The Second Graduation Ceremony was held for 46 Bachelor of Science students on 29th December 2013. As the guests of honour, Her Excellency Maitha Al Mahrouqi, Undersecretary of the Ministry of Tourism was attending the ceremony along with His Excellency Sheikh Abdullah bin Salim Al Salmi, member of the Board of Governors at GUtech, His Excellency Abdullah bin Nasser Al Rahbi, Ambassador at the Permanent Mission of the Sultanate of Oman to the United Nations Office and other international organizations in Geneva, the German Ambassador the the Sultanate of Oman His Excellency Hans-Christian Freiherr von Reibnitz, Director General of Muscat Securities Market (MSM) Mr Ahmed Saleh Al Marhoon, members of the Majlis Al Shura and other dignitaries attended. Dr. Hussain Al Salmi, Vice-Rector for Administration and Finance, mentioned in his speech that most of the graduates have witnessed the early days of GUtech — the GUtech beach campus in Al Athaiba, the relocation to the airport campus and now the final campus in Halban. Although the Halban Campus has received several architectural awards Dr. Hussain stressed that the building is not as important as the students and their knowledge acquired. 'Education is the passport to the future, and not to the good life only, but to change the world to be better,' said Dr. Hussain Al Salmi. On behalf of all graduates Talal Ziad Al Haremi expressed their gratitude to the 'GUtech family'. He encouraged the other graduates to realise their own ideas. 'Follow your dreams, no matter what it takes,' he said. The ceremony concluded with forty-six white and blue balloons flying off into the sky.

2013
APPLIED GEOSCIENCES

Nutaila Al Shaibani

Alya Al Maskiry

Zeena Al Naamani

Ahad Al Zadjali

Shamsa Al Batrani

Mohammed Al Shamli

Rihab Al Yaarubi

Khalda Al Barwani

Yasmeen Al Shaqsi

Jokha Al Thanawi

Areej Al Ghaithi

2013
APPLIED INFORMATION TECHNOLOGY

Ahmed Al Naamani

Haitham Farah

Al Harith Al Jamali

Anas Al Sulaimi

Mohibullah Kamal

2013
URBAN PLANNING AND ARCHITECTURE

Iman Al Ajmi

Shaima Al Raisi

Taleed Rose

Al Israa Al Saadi

Mahir Al Arafati

Talal Al Haremi

Ricky Vinayachandran

Maryam Al Taei

Amr Al Zadjali

Nibras Al Malahi

Noor Al Raisi

Sabreen Al Baddaii

Sultan Al Zadjali

Asila Al Busaidi

Asiya Al Lamki

Khadija Al Mandhari

Saleh Al Adawy

Rola Al Harthy

Shatha Al Mazrouai

Maiysa Al Mandhari

Fatma Al Rahbi

Hamida Al Riyami

Hanan Al Riyami

Mohammed Al Madhani

Nasser Al Sayegh

Fouz Al Busaidi

Sabrina Sultan

Ayesha Akhtar

Nadeen Al Tall

FIG. 127/13:
View of the Amphitheatre during
the Graduation Ceremony.

FIG. 128/13: Above left: GUtech Vice-Rector Administration and Finance Dr. Hussain Al Salmi.

FIG. 129/13: Above right: GUtech Rector Prof. Dr. Modigell presenting the graduation certificate to UPAD graduate Nadeen Al Tall.

FIG. 130/13: Below: Graduation Ceremony 2013.

2014

THIRD GRADUATION CEREMONY

The 3rd Graduation Ceremony for a total of 56 students in the large GUtech auditorium was held on January 4th 2015. His Highness Sayyid Faisal bin Turki Al Said and the German Ambassador the the Sultanate of Oman His Excellency Hans-Christian Freiherr von Reibnitz, His Excellency Sheikh Abdullah bin Salim Al Salmi, member of the Board of Governors at GUtech as well as members of the Majlis Al Shura and other dignitaries attended the ceremony, together with a large number family members of GUtech graduates, GUtech students, staff. The Rector advised the GUtech graduates to choose their future work wisely, based on their talents rather than on the salary, 'in harmony with your minds and hearts. In the end success will bring you a higher salary,' he said. On behalf of the GUtech graduates Fathiya Al Kindi, a graduate of the Department of Sustainable Tourism and Development (STRD) said: 'This is one of our most important days in our lives.' Fathiya compared the studies with a journey, which was not always smooth but with a great result. She thanked all parents for supporting them and being their backbones. She also thanked the professors, who 'have awakened our expectations and inspired us to widen our horizon.'

2014
APPLIED GEOSCIENCES

Maha Al Rawahi

Nawras Al Heraki

Basim Al Rahbi

Ahmed Al Hasani

Hamed Al Sheibani

Mohammed Al Senani

Moza Al Balushi

Nawwar Al Sinawi

Waqar Akram

Safaa Al Habsi

Mataz Al Abri

2014
COMPUTER SCIENCE

Sabra Al Busaidi

Lubna Al Ma'awali

Haitham Al Mawali

Sharifa Al Farsi

Naheed Al Quraishi

Thunaiya Al Habsi

Issa Al Rawahi

Abdullah Shams

Nada Al Amri

Mahmuda Ayman

Hisham Abdulaziz

2014
SUSTAINABLE TOURISM AND REGIONAL DEVELOPMENT

Asya Al Naamani

Reem Al Kalbani

Al Anood Al Mohamed

Alla Al Habsi

Shurooq Al Hashmi

Fathiya Al Kindi

2014
URBAN PLANNING AND ARCHITECTURAL DESIGN

Hamed Al Brashdi

Amal Al Kalbani

Jokha Al Harthy

Nujaida Al Maskari

Aya Al Balushi

Iram Al Hamdani

Rujaina Al Kitani

Ala Al Kendi

Azza Al Kindi

Buthainah Jandal

Amna Al Sharji

Nauras Al Malahi

Orjuwan Al Bulushi

Nasir Mamun

Tasneem Khaleque

Michaela Schweizer

Shaharin Annisa

Nora Al Hinai

Haya Al Bawwab

Muzn Bahram

Worood Bahwan

FIG. 131/14:
Graduation 2014.
Computer Science
Graduate Mahmuda
Ayman taking an
oath on being an
active ambassador for
GUtech and using the
acquired knowledge
for the comunitiy.

FIG. 132/14:
Graduation 2014.
The Rectorate and
Members of the
Faculties.

FIG. 133/14:
Rector Prof. Dr. Michael Modigell presenting the Bachelor Certificate to 2014 Computer Science Graduate Issa Al Rawahi.

FIG. 134/14:
Graduation 2014. UPAD graduate addressing the audience.

FIG. 135/14:
Graduation 2014.
Group Photo.

2015

FOURTH GRADUATION CEREMONY

During the 4th Graduation Ceremony, a total of 66 graduates were celebrated on the 13th of December 2015. The ceremony was attended by the Ambassador of the Federal Republic of Germany to the Sultanate, members of the Board of Governors at GUtech, members of the Majlis Al Dowla and Majlis Al Shura as well as other dignitaries. For the first time students graduated from the BEng in Mechanical Engineering and Process Engineering programmes. Ahlam Al Mutawa and Arwa Al Marhoobi addressed the audience on behalf of the GUtech graduate students. 'Graduates of 2015, we have made it' said Ahlam while continuing to thank for all support received from parents, friends and family members. 'We were taught not what to think but how to think,' she said adding that many students participated in study-excursions to different places, for example to Germany, to Spain, UK or elsewhere. 'Most of us got the privilege to travel to Germany which helped us to mature in our studies.'

2015
APPLIED GEOSCIENCES

Noof Al Hinaai

Maryam Al Naamani

Saleem Al Shukairi

Bushra Al Quraishi

Maryam Al Balushi

Muzna Al Zadjali

Shahla Al Mahrooqi

Samira Al Balushi

Amira Al Saifi

Ahmed Al Taan

Saleh Al Ismaili

Saif Bawany

2015
COMPUTER SCIENCE

Shaima Al Wahaibi

Fatema Al Bahri

Arwa Al Marhoobi

Samiha Al Habsi

Sabha Al Maskari

Rehab Al Dhawyani

Maroa Al Aasmi

Zahra Al Lawati

Marwa Al Harthy

Nusaiba Al Sulaimani

Ahlam Al Mutawa

Narjes Jamali

2015
MECHANICAL ENGINEERING

Ahmed Al Azizi

Mohammad Mohammadifar

Ishaq Al Busaidi

Mohammed Omer

Yazeed Al Ghafri

Azeem Noor Khan

Mobashar Kabir
Humayan Kabir

Shehab Hassan

Fahmi Al Habsi

Dibin Jossey

2015
PROCESS ENGINEERING

Hawraa Al Maimani   Rawan Al Yaarubi   Shadha Al Asfoor   Ali Sabt   Abdullah Al Riyami

2015
URBAN PLANNING AND ARCHITECTURE

Fatema Al Rashdi

Ahmed Al Ruzaiqi

Samah Al Farsi

Faye Abdullah

Hadi Al Muscati

Khoula Al Salmi

Mohamed Al Zadjali

Maram Al Balushi

Habiba Al Shaqsi

Safa Al Shukairy

Hawa Al Harrasi

Fatma Al Harrasi

Aseel Elagib

Widad Al Shakaili

Yomna Mohamed

Nikhil Cherian

Muhammad Al Timami

Yasir Otbi

Sulaiman Al Harthy

Miriam Osman

Manal Al Hajri

2015
SUSTAINABLE TOURISM AND REGIONAL DEVELOPMENT

Yusra Al Kindi

Flavia Mendes

Aryana Al Hamdani

Azhar Al Shukaili

Jokha Al Suqri

Sulayma Al Jahdhami

Siham Al Mabsly

Tasnim Al Nasseri

FIG. 136/15: Above left: Master of Ceremony Namariq Al Zadjali addressing the audience.

FIG. 137/15: Above right: Graduation 2015. Group Photo.

FIG. 138/15: Graduates 2015.

2016

FIFTH GRADUATION CEREMONY

The 5th Graduation Ceremony was held on 11th December 2016, when a total of 69 graduates, 42 females and 27 males, were celebrated during an official ceremony held in the auditorium of the campus in Barka. Rama Alakad, who studied Urban Planning and Architectural Design (UPAD) said on behalf of all graduates, that the Graduation is an exceptional day in their lives but that 'education does not have an end'. Rama thanked all their professors and families who contributed to their successful studies. Rama added: 'GUtech was our second home. I never felt alone. We were always there for each other.'

2016
APPLIED GEOSCIENCES

Yasser Al Nabhani

Ahmed Al Ghallabi

Reem Al Tuqi

Dayana Al Balushi

Atheer Al Jahdhami

Jamla Al Jabri

Sabra Al Shaqsi

Reem Moosani

Zuwaina Al Harthy

Fadwa Al Zadjali

Atiya Al Sabahi

Zamzam Al Qasmi

Al Muhanna Al Harthi

Harith Al Kubaisy

Ahlam Al Jabri

Noor Al Araji

2016
MECHANICAL ENGINEERING

Queiss Al Maskri

Anas Bendari

Balaj Fazal

Mustafa Al Ajmi

Nayan Nath

Ahmad Khan

Muhammad Atif Nawaz

Abdurrahman Umar

2016
PROCESS ENGINEERING

Marwa Al Hinai

Balqees Al Maamari

Lubna Al Riyami

Siham Al Yousfi

Maryam Al Mukhaini

Hajir Al Dhawi

Zahra Al Ajmi

Noor Al Abri

Bashair Al Sa'idi

Balqees Al Siyabi

Jawaher Al Zadjaliv

Raiya Al Aisri

Sumaiya Al Battashi

Ali Sufian

Mustafa Al Hinai

Faisal Al Busaidi

Shaima Abdul Wahab

Zainab Al Mamari

Talal Al Busaidi

Mahmood Al Ruqaishi

2016
URBAN PLANNING AND ARCHITECTURE

Marwa Al Khusaibi

Muhaina Al Khusaibi

Maisa Al Rawahi

Ibrahim Al Manthari

Mohammed Al Sharji

Salma Al Balushi

Ahmed Al Sharji

Jamilah Qattan

Yara Al Balushi

Faiza Al Zadjali

Thuraiya Al Balushi

Wijdan Al Kindi

Sami Al Habsi

Majid Al Busaidi

Sultan Al Touqi

2016
URBAN PLANNING AND ARCHITECTURE (PAGE 2)

Yasmeen Abdulla

Rama Alakad

Mohammed Noman

Muhammad Ahmed Bhatti

Thuraiya Al Riyamy

Rifath Rizvee

Alla Al Jashmi

Rawan Bassett

Tauseef Ahmed

FIG. 139/16: Above left:
2016 Engineering Graduates.

FIG. 140/16: Above right:
Graduation 2016. Group Photo.

FIG. 141/16: Below:
Graduation 2016. Group Photo.

2017

SIXTH GRADUATION CEREMONY

GUtech held its 6th Graduation Ceremony along with the 10th anniversary of the university on 10th December 2017. A total of 115 students graduated officially that day. 'We are proud of our graduates. Several graduates have conducted their Bachelor thesis in Engineering, Geosciences and Urban Planning and Architectural Design at our partner-universities in Germany, RWTH Aachen and University of Erlangen, or in Italy, the University of Brescia. We are happy that our students are increasingly interested in going abroad to widen their horizons and at the same time increase their future job perspectives,' said Prof. Dr. Michael Modigell, Rector of GUtech. Prof. Dr. Wilfried Bauer, Head of Applied Geosciences Department, recalled: "Looking back to the good moments, I would say our field trips were the best. In addition, submission days were always interesting. Shamsa Al Brashdi is a graduate in BSc Applied Geosciences. Shamsa has been pursuing her MSc in Applied Petroleum Geosciences in Edinburgh, Scotland, at Heriott Watt University, the programme is sponsored by Petroleum Development Oman (PDO). 'Geoscience was not my first passion. However, the idea of learning about your own planet and what it hides in the subsurface attracted me. Starting with my first year, I started doubting if this programme was suitable for me or not. I can never, and would never, forget when one of the Professors said this sentence: "Each rock has its own story". This sentence made me love what I'm studying, and that day I was sure that this is what I wanted to do'.

2017
APPLIED GEOSCIENCES

Yusra Al Shoukri

Amur Al Rawas

Hajir Al Taubi

Amani Qasim

Amal Al Shahaibi

Wafa Al Ismaili

Shamsa Al Brashdi

Marwa Al Riyami

Nayila Al Balushi

Ali Al Hajri

Amal Al Zubaidi

Raqiya Al Dhuhli

Salima Al Harthy

Wissal Al Habsi

Ibtisam Al Kharusi

Ghaliya Al Busaidi

2017
COMPUTER SCIENCE

Abeer Al Rahbi

Alya Al Shanfari

Aida Al Harthi

Abdullah Al Farsi

Omar Al Kindi

2017
ENVIRONMENTAL ENGINEERING

Reem Al Maskari

Balqis Al Mazruii

Aisha Al Maani

Khadija Al Balushi

Maryam Al Raisi

Khaloud Al Zaabi

Abeer Al Sulaimi

Hanan Al Habsi

Al Anood Al Hadrami

Manar Al Hamadani

Rageemah Samie

Hajar Al Ruqaishi

2017
MECHANICAL ENGINEERING

Issa Al Habsi

Amjad Al Yaarubi

Moayyad Al Bahrani

Yousef Dak Al Bab

Said Al Dughaishi

Haitham Al Waaili

Anas El Bera

Aisha Al Falahi

Tejas Janardhan

Mohamed Salman

Said Al Ofi

Mohamed Al Busaidi

Ahmed Al Kindi

2017
PROCESS ENGINEERING

Khaloud Al Naqabi

Al Anoud Al Naqabi

Shurooq Al Saidi

Mazin Al Saadi

Hanin Al Mukhaini

Alya Al Siyabi

Wafa Al Saadi

Ruqaiya Al Jawi Al Araimi

Asma Al Alawi

Wafa Al Akhzami

Ali Mansuri

Elham Al Hadhrami

Sheikha Al Hinai

Eman Al Rashdi

Kathiya Al Wardi

Afaf Al Shuhaibi

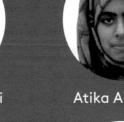
Atika Al Rahbi

Abeer Al Zadjali

Noor Al Balushi

Sara Al Jabri

Fatma Al Aamri

Sumaiya Al Harthi

Malik Al Abri

Sultan Al Shekaili

Abrar Al Mandhari

Nawal Al Amry

Maryam Al Abri

Suhaila Al Bulushi

Fatma Al Aamri

Qusai Al Hajri

Yasmeen Al Thuhli

Samira Al Subhi

Majda Al Kalbani

Al Yaqdhan Al Wardi

Said Al Badwawi

Abdullah Al Rashdi

Basma Al Rashdi

Zuwaina Al Zakwani

Qamariya Al Brashdi

Nasser Al Harmali

Ghadeer Redha

Mohammed Mohammed

Lanah Al Sammarraie

2017
URBAN PLANNING AND ARCHITECTURE

Afra Al Zadjali

Bushra Al Sulaimani

Amira Al Balushi

Wael Al Balushi

Maisaa Al Sharji

Marwa Al Huseini

Zahra Al Hasani

Majda Al Habsi

Afra Al Abri

Amal Al Malki

Maisoon Al Farsi

Hadeer Al Maskary

Anfal Al Zadjali

Umaima Al Bulushi

Fatma Al Harthy

2017
URBAN PLANNING AND ARCHITECTURE (PAGE 2)

Reem Al Shaaibi

Basma Al Shuaibi

Maram Al Hinai

Nasr Al Wahaibi

Doa Ghanem

Amaal Al Zeidi

Sara Al Shuaili

Neveen Al Barwani

Maryam Abdu

Jokha Al Zakwani

Lujayna Ghorab

Rimaaz Al Riyami

Farzana Rimi

Deborah Pandian

Amal Al Balushi

Dana Al Haremi

FIG. 142/17: Above left:
Address by Dr. Hussain Al Salmi.

FIG. 143/17: Above right:
Graduation group photo.

FIG. 144/17:
Rector Prof. Dr. Michael
Modigell presenting the
Bachelor Certificate to
2017 UPAD Graduate
Dana Al Haremi.

FIG. 145/17:
Graduation Ceremony 2017. Group Photo.

APPENDIX

LIST OF AUTHORS

- **Dr. Christian Bode**, Former Secretary General of the German Academic Exchange Service DAAD; member of GUtech Board of Governors (BoG) since 2007

- **Univ.- Prof. em. Dr. rer. nat. Günter Flügge**, Chair of Experimental Physics of RWTH Aachen University 1986–2005; Physics Course Coordinator of the Foundation Programme 2007–2010

- **Univ.- Prof. Adj. Prof. (GUtech) Dr. rer. nat. Martina Fromhold-Eisebith**, Chair of Economic Geography of RWTH Aachen University since 2006; Inaugural Dean of the Faculty of Economics and Tourism Development 2007–2012 and Adjunct Professor of GUtech since 2012

- **His Excellency Klaus Geyer**, German Ambassador to the Sultanate of Oman 2006–2009

- **Dr. rer. nat. Manuela Gutberlet**, Public Relations Manager of GUtech since 2007

- **Univ.- Prof. Dr. rer. nat. Christoph Hilgers**, Chair of Structural Geology of Karlruhe Institute of Technology (KIT); GUtech Deputy Rector for Administration and Finance 2007–2009

- **His Excellency Dr. Hilal Al Hinai**, Secretary General of The Research Council of Oman (TRC)

- **Arch. Ernst Höhler**, Founder of Höhler+Partner Architekten und Ingenieure and Co-Founder of Hoehler + Partner (H+P), rebranded to Hoehler + alSalmy (H+S), Architects and Engineers in 2016

- **Prof. em. Heiner Hoffmann**, Chair of Design of RWTH Aachen University; Professor of Creative Design Foundation Courses of GUtech 2007–2010

- **Myriam Hoffmann**, Instructor of the Creative Design Foundation Courses of GUtech 2007–2010

- **Manfred von Holtum**, Provost of Aachen Cathedral since 2014

- **Univ.-Prof. em. Prof. (GUtech) Dr.-Ing. habil. Michael Jansen**, Chair of History of Urbanization of RWTH Aachen University 1987–2012; Vice Rector Teaching of RWTH Aachen University 1997–1999; Acting Rector of GUtech 2007–2008; Member of GUtech Board of Governors (BoG) 2007–2012, Full Professor of GUtech since 2012; Establishment of Research Centre Indian Ocean (RIO) at GUtech

- **Univ.-Prof. em. Adj. Prof. (GUtech) Dr. rer. nat. Matthias Jarke**, Chair of Databases and Information Systems of RWTH Aachen 1991–2021; Executive Director, Fraunhofer Institute of Applied Information Technology FIT 2000–2021, Germany; Inaugural Dean of the Faculty of Engineering 2007–2012 and Adjunct Professor of GUtech since 2012

- **Bruno Kaiser**, President of the German-Omani Association, Berlin

- **Dr. iur. Jürgen Linden**, Former Lord Mayor of Aachen 1989–2009

- **Univ.- Prof. em. Dr. rer. nat. Michael Modigell**, Chair of Mechanical Process Engineering of RWTH Aachen University; Rector of GUtech 2013–2020

- **Dr. Heinrich Mussinghoff**, Bishop Emeritus of Aachen Diocese 1994–2015

- **Manfred Nettekoven**, Chancellor and Head of Administration and Finance of RWTH Aachen University since 2006

- **Dr. h.c. W. Georg Olms**, Publisher Olms Verlag, Hildesheim

- **Prof. em. Roshdi Rashed**, Em. Research Director (distinguished class) of the National Centre for Scientific Research CNRS, Paris 7 University; Honorary Professor of the University of Tokyo; Professor em. of the University of Mansourah (Egypt)

- **Univ.- Prof. em. Dr. rer. nat. Dr. h.c. Burkhard Rauhut**, Chair of Mathematical Statistics and Business Mathematics of RWTH Aachen University 1973–1999; Rector of RWTH Aachen University 1999–2008; Rector of GUtech 2008–2013

- **His Excellency Hans-Christian Freiherr von Reibnitz**, German Ambassador to the Sultanate of Oman 2012–2017

- **His Excellency Sheikh Abdullah bin Mohammed Al Salmi**, Chairman of Oman Educational Services LLC (OES) since 2007

- **His Excellency Sheikh Abdullah bin Salim Al Salmi**, Member of Oman Educational Services LLC (OES) Executive Board since 2007

- **Dr. Abdulrahman Al Salimi**, Member of Oman Educational Services LLC (OES) Executive Board since 2007

- **Dr. Hussain Al Salmi**, Deputy Rector of GUtech for Administration and Finance since 2009; CEO of Oman Educational Services LLC (OES) since 2016; Acting Rector of GUtech since 2020

- **Arch. Muhammad bin Sultan Al Salmy**, Co-Founder, Managing Partner and Lead Architect at Hoehler + alSalmy (H+S), previously (until 2016) Hoehler + Partner (H+P)

- **Univ.- Prof. Dr. rer. nat. Ernst Schmachtenberg**, Rector of RWTH Aachen University 2008–2018; Chairman of GUtech Board of Governors 2008–2018

- **Univ.-Prof. Dr.-Ing. Robert Schmitt**, Representative of the Rector's Office of RWTH Aachen for Cooperation with the Arab Gulf States; Member of GUtech Board of Governors since 2007

- **His Excellency Thomas Friedrich Schneider,** German Ambassador to the Sultanate of Oman 2017–present

- **Prof. (GUtech) Dr. rer. nat. Barbara Stäuble**, Deputy Rector of GUtech for Academic Affairs 2007–2012

- **Her Excellency Angelika Storz-Chakarji**, German Ambassador to the Sultanate of Oman 2009–2012

- **Dr. iur. Michael Stückradt**, Chancellor and Head of Administration and Finance of RWTH Aachen University 2000–2005; Chancellor of University of Cologne since 2010

- **Univ.-Prof. Adj. Prof. (GUtech) Dr. rer. nat. Janos Urai**, Chair of Structural Geology, Tectonics and Geomechanics of RWTH Aachen University since 2006; Inaugural Dean of the Faculty of Sciences 2007–2012 and Adjunct Professor of GUtech since 2012

- **Apl.- Prof. em. Adj. Prof. (GUtech) Rolf Westerheide**, Department of Urban Design and Regional Planning of RWTH Aachen University 2006–2018; Inaugural Dean of the Faculty of Urban Planning and Architectural Design 2007–2012 and Adjunct Professor of GUtech since 2012

- **Univ.- Prof. em. Dr. Margret Wintermantel**, Chair of Social Psychology of Saarland University 1992–2000; Rector of Saarland University 2000–2006; President of German Rectors Conference 2006–2012; President of the German Academic Exchange Service DAAD since 2012

وزارة التعليم العالى

قرار وزارى

رقم ٩ / ٢٠٠٧

بانشاء الجامعة العمانية الألمانية للتكنولوجيا

استنادا إلى المرسوم السلطانى رقم ٩٩/٤١ بإصدار نظام الجامعات الخاصة ،

وإلى القرار الوزارى رقم ٩٩/٣٦ بإصدار اللائحة التنفيذية لنظام الجامعات الخاصة ،

وإلى قرار مجلس التعليم العالى رقم ٢٠٠٦/١/١١ ،

وبناء على ما تقتضيه المصلحة العامة .

تقـرر

مـادة (١) : تنشأ جامعة خاصة تسمى (الجامعة العمانية الألمانية للتكنولوجيا) ، تكون لها الشخصية الاعتبارية ، وتضم كلية الهندسة وكلية العلوم وكلية تكنولوجيا المعلومات والرياضيات وكلية الاقتصاد والتخطيط ويكون مقرها الرئيسى محافظة مسقط .

مـادة (٢) : تخضع الجامعة لأحكام نظام الجامعات الخاصة المشار إليه ولائحته التنفيذية ، ويمثلها رئيسها أمام الغير .

مـادة (٣) : يمنح المؤسسون مدة ستة أشهر اعتبارا من تاريخ العمل بهذا القرار ، لإنهاء الإجراءات اللازمة لممارسة الجامعة أعمالها ، ويصدر ببدء الدراسة بالجامعة قرار من وزيرة التعليم العالى .

مـادة (٤) : تصدر جماعة المؤسسين قرارا بتشكيل أول مجلس لأمناء الجامعة وذلك على النحو المنصوص عليه فى نظام الجامعات الخاصة المشار إليه .

مـادة (٥) : يتولى مجلس أمناء الجامعة المهام والاختصاصات المبينة بنظام الجامعات الخاصة ، وعلى الأخص تعيين رئيس الجامعة ونوابه وأعضاء مجلس الجامعة .

مـادة (٦) : يشكل مجلس الجامعة برئاسة رئيسها وعضوية نوابه وعمداء الكليات ورؤساء مراكز البحوث العلمية ، ويجوز أن يضم المجلس أعضاء من الشخصيات العامة من ذوى الخبرة فى شؤون التعليم يعينهم مجلس الأمناء .

مـادة (٧) : يختص مجلس الجامعة بالإضافة إلى مهامه الأخرى بما يأتى :

١ – تسيير الشؤون العلمية والإدارية للجامعة وتنفيذ السياسات التى يقررها مجلس الأمناء .

٢ – إقرار سياسات وشروط قبول الطلاب بكل كلية .

٣ – تنظيم شؤون خدمات الطلاب الثقافية والرياضية والاجتماعية .

٤ – تحديد قواعد اختيار العمداء ومجالس الكليات ومراكز البحوث العلمية .

٥ – اقتراح خطة الدراسة ومواعيد بدايتها ونهايتها ونظام الفصول الدراسية .

٦ – وضع نظم المحاضرات والبحوث والتمرينات العملية ونظم الامتحانات .

٧ – دراسة وإبداء الرأى فى المسائل الأخرى التى يحيلها إليه مجلس الأمناء .

٨ – تقوية الروابط بين الجامعة والجامعات الأخرى والمعاهد العلمية والبحثية المختلفة والجهات الحكومية .

مـادة (٨) : يكون لكل كلية عميد ومساعد للعميد ومجلس للكلية يشكل برئاسة العميد ، وعضوية مساعده ورؤساء الأقسام .

مـادة (٩) : يختص مجلس الكلية بتسيير الشؤون العلمية والإدارية بالكلية ، وبصفة خاصة ما يأتى :

١ – إقرار المحتوى العلمى لمقررات الدراسة فى الكلية .

٢ – تحديد مواعيد الامتحانات ووضع جداولها وتوزيع أعمالها وتشكيل لجانها .

٣ – اقتراح تعيين أعضاء هيئات التدريس ، وندبهم .

Sultanate of Oman

Ministry of Higher Education

Office of the Minister

سلطنة عمان
وزارة التعليم العالي
مكتب الوزير

٤ – اقتراح نظم المحاضرات ، والتمرينات العملية .

٥ – دراسة وإبداء الرأي في المسائل الأخرى التي يحيلها إليه مجلس الجامعة .

مـادة (١٠) : يكون لكل قسم من أقسام الكلية مجلس يتألف من رئيس القسم وعضوية جميع أعضاء هيئة التدريس فيه .

مـادة (١١) : يختص مجلس القسم بالنظر في جميع الشؤون العلمية والدراسية والإدارية المتعلقة بالقسم ، وعلى الأخص بما يأتى :

١ – وضع نظام العمل بالقسم ، والتنسيق بين مختلف التخصصات .

٢ – تحديد المقررات الدراسية التي يتولى القسم تدريسها وتحديد محتواها العلمي .

٣ – تحديد الكتب والمراجع في مواد القسم وتيسير حصول الطلاب عليها .

٤ – مناقشة التقرير السنوى لرئيس القسم .

مـادة (١٢) : تقبل الجامعة الطلاب العمانيين والأجانب الحاصلين على الشهادة العامة أو ما يعادلها وفقا لشروط القبول التي يحددها مجلس الجامعة .

مـادة (١٣) : تمنح الجامعة بعد موافقة الوزارة الدرجات العلمية الواردة في الإطار الوطنى للمؤهلات العلمية .

مـادة (١٤) : ينشر هذا القرار في الجريدة الرسمية ، ويعمل به من تاريخ نشره .

صدر فى : ١٢ محرم ١٤٢٨هـ

الموافق : ٣١ يناير ٢٠٠٧م

د . راوية بنت سعود البوسعيدية

وزيــرة التعليــم العالــى

ــــــــــــــــــــــ

قرار وزاري رقم (٧٠/٢٠٠٨)

استناداً إلى المرسوم السلطاني رقم ٢٠٠٢/٦ بتحديد اختصاصات وزارة التعليم العالي واعتماد هيكلها التنظيمي،

وإلى القرار الوزاري رقم ٢٠٠٧/٩ بإنشاء الجامعة العُمانية الألمانية للتكنولوجيا،

وبناءً على ما تقتضيه مصلحة العمل.

تقـــــرر

مادة(١) : يعـدل مسمى الجامعـة العُمانيـة الألمانية للتكنولوجيا إلى الجامعـة الألمانيـة للتكنولوجيا في عُمان.

مادة (٢): يلغى كــل مــا يخالــف هــذا القرار أو يتـــعــارض مع أحــكامه.

مادة (٣): ينشر هــذا القرار بالجريـدة الرسمية ويعمل بـه اعتباراً من تاريخ نشره.

د.راوية بنت سعود البوسعيدية
وزيــرة التعليــم العالي

صدر فى : ١٥ جمادى الأولى ١٤٢٩هـ
الموافق : ٢١ مايـــو ٢٠٠٨م

Approval by Ministry of Higher Education (MoHE) MD No 9/2007 dated 31 January 2007 and MD NO. 70/2008 DATED 15 JUNE 2008 for the establishment of the *Oman German University of Technology* (OGtech) later renamed to *German University of Technology in Oman* (GUtech).

Official gazette No. 835
Dated 17 March 2007
Pages 7 to 9

Ministry of High Education
Ministerial Decision
No. 9/2007
To form the Oman German University of Technology

Based on the Royal Decree No. 41/99 to issue the Private University Rule,

And the Ministerial Decision No. 36/99 to issue the Executive Regulation of the Private University Rule,

And the High Educational Council's Decision No. 11/1/2006,

And in accordance with the exigencies of the public good.

Decided

Article (1): A private university shall be formed under the name of (Oman German University of Technology), and shall have a juristic person, and shall include a Faculty of Engineering, a Faculty of Science, a Faculty of Mathematics and Information Technology and a Faculty of Economics and Planning, and the location of its head office shall be in the Muscat Governorate.

Article (2): The University shall be subject to the provisions of the Private Universities Rule referred to and its Executive Regulation, and shall be represented by its Rector before others.

Article (3): The founders shall be granted six months period, effective from the date this decision shall come into force, to complete the procedures necessary for the University to practise its business, and a decision by the Minister of High Education shall be issued for the commencement of the study in the University.

Article (4): The group of founders shall issue a decision to form the first Board of Trustees for the University, in accordance with the Private Universities Rule referred to.

Article (5): The University's Board of Trustees shall assume the functions and the authorities shown in the Private Universities Rule, and in particular appoint a Rector for the University, his deputies and the University Council members.

Article (6): The University Council shall be chaired by the Rector of the University, his deputies, the Deans of the Faculties and the Heads of the Scientific Research Centres. The University Council may include members from the public, personalities who are having experience in educational affairs and shall be appointed by the Board of Trustees.

Article (7): In addition to its other functions, the University Council shall be specialised in the following:
1 Manage the scientific and administrative affairs of the University and execute the policies which are decided by the Board of Trustees.
2 Approve the policies and conditions of accepting students in the University.
3 Organise the students services affairs related to education, sports and social.
4 Determine the basis to select deans, faculty boards and scientific research centres.
5 Recommend a study plan, and deadline for its commencement and its end and the study terms rule.
6 Set up the rule for lectures, research, practical exercises and examination rules.
7 Study and express an opinion on the other issues which are transferred by the Board of Trustees.
8 Enhance the relationship between the University and other universities, various scientific and research institutions and governments authorities.

Article (8): Each faculty shall have a dean, assistant dean and a faculty board, which will be chaired by the dean, the assistant-deans and the heads of departments.

Article (9): The faculty board shall be specialised in managing the scientific and administrative affairs of the college, and in particular the following:
1 Approve the scientific contents of the stipulated education in the college.
2 Determine the examination dates, set up its schedules, distribute its work and form its committees.
3 Recommend appointing the educational authorities members, and appoint them.

4   Recommend the rules of lectures and practical exercises.

5   Study and express an opinion on the other issues which are transferred by the University Council.

Article (10):   Each department within a faculty shall have a board which is composed of the Head of Department and all the academic staff in the department.

Article (11):   The department board is specialised in looking into all the scientific, educational and administrative affairs related to the division, and in particular in the following:

1   Set up a work rule in the department, and liaise between the different specialisations.

2   Determine the educational curriculum which the department shall be responsible for teaching and determine its scientific contents.

3   Determine the books and references for the subjects of the division and facilitate for the students to obtain them.

4   Discuss the annual report of the Head of Department.

Article (12):   The University shall accept Omani and foreign students who have obtained general education certificate or its equivalent in accordance with the entry requirements which are determined by the University Council.

Article (13):   After the approval of Ministry, the University shall grant the scientific grades mentioned in the national context of the scientific qualifications.

Article (14):   This decision shall be published in the official gazette, and shall come into force from date of its publication.

Issued on 31 January 2007

Dr. Rawya bint Saoud Al Busaidia
Minister of High Education

Ministerial Decision No. 70/2008 issued by Ministry of Higher Education published in the official gazette No. 865 on **15 June 2008**.

Article 1: The name of Oman German University of Technology shall be amended to the German University of Technology in Oman.

Article 2: Any provision which violates or contradicts this decision shall be cancelled.

Article 3: This decision shall be published in the official gazette, and shall come into force effective from date of its publication (**15 June 2008**).

Issued on 21 May 2008

Dr. Rawya bint Saoud Al-Bousaidi
Minister of Higher Education

Translation